Migration and Population

ISSUES

Volume 150

Editors

Cobi Smith and Lisa Firth

Educational Publishers
Cambridge

First published by Independence
The Studio, High Green
Great Shelford
Cambridge CB22 5EG
England

Copyright

Photocopy licence

British Library Cataloguing in Publication Data

Migration and Population – (Issues Series)
I. Smith, Cobi II. Series
363.9

ISBN 978 1 86168 423 3

Printed in Great Britain

MWL Print Group Ltd

Cover

The illustration on the front cover is by Simon Kneebone.

CONTENTS

Chapter One: Migration and Security

Chapter Two: Population

Useful information for readers

Dear Reader,

Issues: Migration and Population

Migration is not a new phenomenon, but it is one which increasingly hits the headlines. It is highly controversial, with some believing the UK is too open to migrants, resulting in negative consequences for the current population, and others defending migrants as beneficial to our economy. Meanwhile, the population of the UK and the world continues to grow amid fears about sustainability. Is there a solution to the problem?

The purpose of *Issues*

Migration and Population is the one hundred and fiftieth volume in the **Issues** series. The aim of this series is to offer up-to-date information about important issues in our world. Whether you are a regular reader or new to the series, we do hope you find this book a useful overview of the many and complex issues involved in the topic.

Titles in the **Issues** series are resource books designed to be of especial use to those undertaking project work or requiring an overview of facts, opinions and information on a particular subject, particularly as a prelude to undertaking their own research.

The information in this book is not from a single author, publication or organisation; the value of this unique series lies in the fact that it presents information from a wide variety of sources, including:

- ⇨ Government reports and statistics
- ⇨ Newspaper articles and features
- ⇨ Information from think-tanks and policy institutes
- ⇨ Magazine features and surveys
- ⇨ Website material
- ⇨ Literature from lobby groups and charitable organisations.*

Critical evaluation

Because the information reprinted here is from a number of different sources, readers should bear in mind the origin of the text and whether the source is likely to have a particular bias or agenda when presenting information (just as they would if undertaking their own research). It is hoped that, as you read about the many aspects of the issues explored in this book, you will critically evaluate the information presented. It is important that you decide whether you are being presented with facts or opinions. Does the writer give a biased or an unbiased report? If an opinion is being expressed, do you agree with the writer?

Migration and Population offers a useful starting point for those who need convenient access to information about the many issues involved. However, it is only a starting point. Following each article is a URL to the relevant organisation's website, which you may wish to visit for further information.

Kind regards,

Lisa Firth
Editor, **Issues** series

** Please note that Independence Publishers has no political affiliations or opinions on the topics covered in the **Issues** series, and any views quoted in this book are not necessarily those of the publisher or its staff.*

Migration guide

Information from OneWorld.net

Migration is not a recent phenomenon. For centuries, people have moved across borders for economic and political reasons. Contemporary labour migration, however, is characterised by its feminisation, its temporary nature, its poor working conditions, and frequent abuses and violations of human rights. Considered as second-class citizens, often relegated to 3D (dirty, dangerous, difficult) jobs, many migrant workers are professionals who take on jobs that do not utilise their full skills and potential.

Labour migration: a brief overview

Over the past decade, international migration has been growing as a consequence of the increasing integration of world economies and the changing needs in both the countries of destination and the countries of origin. According to the UN Population Division, there are now almost 200 million inter-national migrants.

In October 2005, the Global Commission on International Migration (GCIM) released its final report, *Migration in an interconnected world: New directions for action*. The commissioners write that: 'the international community has failed to realise the full potential of international migration and has not risen to the many opportunities and challenges it presents'. In response, the UN held its first ever high level plenary on migration in September 2006, focusing on a report by Kofi Annan titled 'International Migration and Development'. The outcome is a new policy advisory group, The Global Forum on Migration and Development, which will hold its first meeting in Brussels in July 2007.

Migration policies are increasingly seen as inherent to a global approach to the monitoring and management of migratory flows, both irregular and regular. In its *World Migration Report 2005*, the International Organization for Migration (IOM) writes that many concerns that surround migration, such as loss of jobs, lower wages, increased welfare costs and the belief that migration is spiralling out of control, are not only exaggerated or unfounded but contrary to evidence.

The International Labour Organisation (ILO) argues that a rights-based international regime for migration management must rest on a framework of principles of good governance, developed and implemented by the international community and acceptable to all. A similar position is taken by UNESCO, which states that human rights should be at the core of any approach to human mobility.

The situation today in the European Union shows the complexity of migration issues. There is the danger of the debate becoming phrased in terms of cultural conflicts and growing fundamentalism versus the increasing need to bring in both low-skilled as well as high-skilled workers. Furthermore, there is the realisation that in the not so distant future Europe's own workforce will most likely be insufficient to support existing social protection mechanisms, primarily the result of an ageing population. The European Commission – and especially the Commissioner for Justice, Freedom and Security – is developing a whole range of interventions that should lead to a new common migration policy covering integration, economic migration, and family reunification.

Global trends

Major Asian countries of destination are Japan, South Korea, Taiwan, Malaysia, Thailand, India and the Arab countries in the Middle East. In the latter, the labour force comprises up to 80% migrant workers. The major sending countries are Philippines, Indonesia, Sri Lanka, Nepal and Bangladesh. The Scalabrini Migration Center publishes *Asian Migration News* providing updates on the situation in Asia. While many Latin Americans used to migrate to Argentina, today many Argentinians and Ecuadorians leave for Spain or Italy and other destinations. Whereas in the 1980s most workers in the south of the US came from Mexico, today they come from all over Latin America. This change transformed Mexico into both a transit country and a country of destination, whilst it also remains a sending country. Other Central American countries also follow this trend, such as Guatemala. The American Friends Services Committee has warned about the negative impact of free trade agreements which drive down labour standards and undermine support for the basic rights and dignity of both documented and undocumented migrant workers. For example, rural workers in Mexico have been forced to migrate in search of employment as small farm agriculture could not compete with the large US corporations. At the same time, the US government is contemplating controversial legislation to prevent undocumented migrants from crossing the border.

In Africa, temporary labour migration, brain drain and unauthorised migration are increasing in scope with large numbers of African workers moving to either South Africa or the European Union. The *Mediterranean Migration 2005* report looks at patterns of migration from and to 10 countries on the Middle East and North African rim of the Mediterranean. It confirms that emigration from these areas is growing, although it points out that fewer than half first-generation migrants go to Europe.

All this makes the protection of documented and undocumented migrants a priority in order to ensure respect for their rights at every stage of their journey, and strengthen social cohesion in the receiving countries.

Feminisation

Half of all international migrants are women, often leaving their children and families behind, and mostly engaged as domestic labour. Since the beginning of the 1980s, there has been a change in trend; women are in greater demand in certain sectors in their countries of destination meaning that they are pushed to go abroad to find a job. A significant number of these women are undocumented migrants, a group to which the trade unions are increasingly giving a voice. The International Confederation of Free Trade Unions (ICFTU) writes that feminisation of migration essentially means that more women are migrating alone whereas previously they would accompany their spouses or join them later. Often hidden within private households, these migrants are even more vulnerable. Sexual abuse, rape, slavery-like labour conditions, and discrimination of all kinds are very common.

Remittances, development and brain drain

More and more, researchers as well as migrant rights activists point to the development potential of international migration. Remittances are probably the most visible aspect, with the World Bank in its *Global Economic Prospects 2006* stating that the officially recorded remittances worldwide have reached US$ 232 billion in 2005, more than double the amount of foreign aid to developing countries for that year. Despite the emphasis on remittances sent from developed countries to developing countries, there is also a significant South-South transfer. The 2006 Kofi Annan report suggests that about one-third of global migrants have moved from one developing country to another. The report advocates policies which stimulate the potential for migration to benefit all parties involved – receiving and sending countries and the migrant families themselves. The linkages established between migrants living abroad and the communities back home open up opportunities for trade, investment, and transfer of skills. In the US, for example, migrants' organisations such as the so-called Home Town Associations pool funds from members to send home for financing community development projects.

There is nevertheless a negative impact from the steady flow of skilled workers from developing countries to North America, Europe and Japan. This is especially the case in the health sector, which is highlighted by ID21 in a study on the effects of the brain drain on health systems in Africa.

Legal protection

The absence of legal routes for migration has led to a significant expansion in human trafficking and smuggling networks which are both dangerous and exploitative in nature. For the majority of would-be migrants, these routes represent the only way to enter an industrialised state.

Although the protection of migrant workers is first of all the duty of both the state of origin and the receiving state, limits of jurisdiction severely curtail the possibility for the state of origin to ensure that its nationals are protected while working abroad. The receiving state, on the other hand, often extends only minimum protection to allow for a flexible labour supply and to avoid social costs. Too often, no labour protection legislation exists for non-nationals and unions are prohibited.

The 2006 Kofi Annan report has been criticised by Human Rights Watch for its focus on development rather than the lack of enforceable rights of migrants. But the international community has not ignored migration completely. The ILO has established a series of standards for the protection of migrants. In addition, the United Nations adopted in 1990 the International Convention on the Protection of the Rights of All Migrant Workers and Members of Their Families, also known as the Migrant Workers' Convention, which entered into force in June 2003.

One of the major challenges for the coming years is to have the Convention ratified by more countries backed by relevant adaptation of their legislation. In April 2005, a coalition of NGOs launched the International Platform on the Migrant Workers' Convention (IPMWC), with the aim to facilitate the promotion, implementation and monitoring of the Convention.

Since none of the EU member states has signed or ratified the Convention, a number of organisations have established a new European Platform to campaign for ratification and to advocate for a rights-based European migration policy.

International Migrants' Day

In 2000, the United Nations proclaimed 18th December as International Migrants' Day (IMD). This is another important step, offering a rallying point for everyone across the world who is concerned with the protection of migrants. The UN invited all of its member states, intergovernmental and non-governmental organisations to observe this day by disseminating information on human rights and fundamental freedoms of migrants, sharing experiences, and undertaking action to ensure the protection of migrants.

⇨ The above information is reprinted with kind permission December 18 and OneWorld.net. Visit www.oneworld.net or www.december18.net for more information.

British least supportive of immigration

The latest *Financial Times*/Harris Poll (FT/Harris Poll) of adults within five countries in Europe shows that, in general, the French take the *most* supportive stance toward immigration within their country and the British take the *least* supportive stance

The British, for instance, are most likely to believe that there are too many immigrants in their country (76%) compared with the French who are least likely to assert this belief (47%). Along similar lines, the British are most likely to believe that their country's policy toward immigration makes it too easy for migrants to enter the country legally (79%) whilst the French are least likely to assert this belief (42%).

Results also show that whilst majorities of adults across the five countries think that their country should 'regulate the flow' of migrants coming into their countries, the British are more likely than the other countries to believe that only those with special skills should be admitted (40%) and the French are more likely to believe that just about anyone who applies should be admitted (11%).

Finally, the British are more likely than adults among the other four countries to state that immigrants in general have had a negative impact on their country's economy (46%) compared to adults in Spain who are most likely to feel they have had a positive impact (39%).

The British are most likely to believe that there are too many immigrants in their country (76%) compared with the French who are least likely to assert this belief (47%)

Illegal immigration

Italian adults are most likely to regard illegal immigration as a problem for their country (96%). In contrast, German adults are least likely to express this view about their country (74%). Consistent with these findings, the Italians are most likely (among the five countries) to believe that their country should tighten up its border controls (91%), and the Germans are least likely to believe that their country should tighten up its border controls (60%).

When asked 'Should your country offer illegal immigrants a one-time opportunity to remain in the country legally, not offer such an opportunity and step up efforts to identify and deport them, or continue on its current path?' Italians were more likely to say that illegal immigrants should be offered a one-time opportunity to remain in their country legally (49%) whilst Germans (71%) were most likely to suggest not offering such an opportunity and stepping up efforts to identify and deport them.

Note: Percentages may not add up exactly to 100% due to rounding.

October 2006

⇨ The above information is reprinted with kind permission from Harris Interactive. Visit www.harrisinteractive.com for more information.

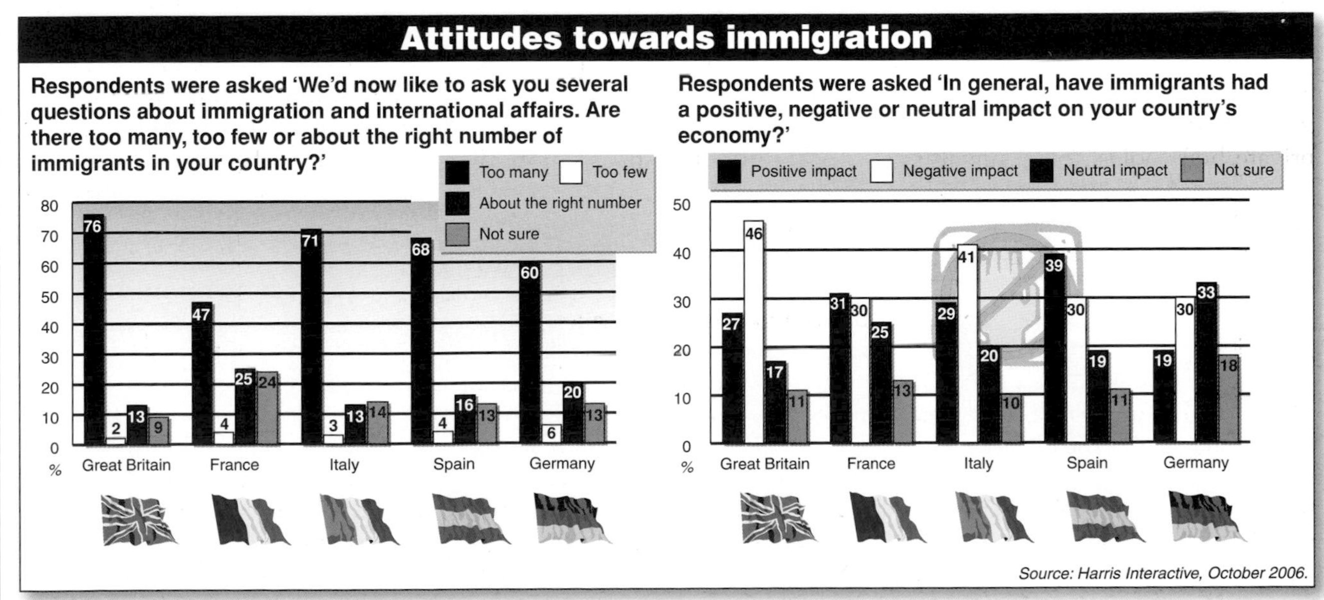

Migration in the UK

Information from the Economic and Social Research Council

Migration defined

The term migration refers to the movement of persons between countries for the purpose of taking up residence. The UK's Office for National Statistics defines a migrant as someone who changes his or her country of residence for a period of at least a year. The terms in-migration and immigration refer to migration into the UK and out-migration or emigration refer to migration out of the UK. Key issues associated with migration, such as asylum, represent a strong concern for economic and social policy in the UK and have in recent times occupied a large proportion of the political agenda.

Migration overview

The International Passenger Survey (IPS) shows that since 1991 there has been an increase in international migration, both in and out of the UK. In 1991, the estimated numbers of in-migrants and out-migrants were roughly similar but since 1994 onwards the numbers of people arriving to live in the UK exceeded the numbers leaving to live elsewhere. In 2005, 185,000 more people entered than left the UK to live for at least a year.

Estimates of Total International Migration (TIM) in 2005, based upon the International Passenger Survey (IPS), showed Australia as the most popular destination for 20 per cent of British out-migrants. Spain and France were the next most popular destinations.

International migration to and from the UK is highest amongst single men and out-migration was highest for the 22-44 age group.

Immigration statistics: key points

As shown in figure 1 below, immigration levels in the UK are rising and have undergone a sharp increase in the years since 1998. In 2005 the estimated number of people arriving to live in the UK for at least a year

was 565,000, an average of over 1,500 a day.

The chart below shows the origin of persons granted settlement in the UK in 2004. The largest proportion of migrants to the UK came from Asia (39 per cent) and Africa (28 per cent). 19 per cent of those granted settlement in the UK originated in Europe. Between 1991 and 2004 the number of acceptances for settlement in the UK more than doubled, rising from 53,900 to 139,260. The persons classified as from 'other' geographical region on the chart include British Overseas Citizens and those whose nationality was unknown.

The majority of settlement grants awarded by the Home Office to migrants in the UK in 2004 were given for reasons of migrants seeking asylum (38 per cent), followed by employment reasons (35 per cent) and family formation and reunion (21 per cent). A further 6 per cent were either unknown or granted on a discretionary basis.

Asylum and immigration

The UK received 40,600 asylum applications in 2004, a fall of 32 per cent from 2003. Figure 3 below shows a comparison between the EU's 15 countries and their asylum applicants, including their dependants.

In 2002 applications to the UK peaked at 103,100, the highest in Europe. When the relative size of the countries' populations are taken into account, the UK ranked tenth in 2004 with 0.7 asylum seekers per 1,000 population. The EU average was 0.6 per 1,000 population and Cyprus had the highest rate at 11.0 per 1,000 population. In comparison the USA received 63,000 asylum claims in 2004 or 0.2 per 1,000 population.

In 2004, 75 per cent of asylum seekers were male and the vast majority were under 35 years (82 per cent). 15 per cent were aged 35 to 49 and only 3 per cent were over 50.

In the third quarter of 2006 the nationality with the most asylum applicants in the UK was Eritrea followed by Afghanistan and Iran. African countries make up half of the top ten application nationalities in the third quarter of 2006.

Immigration levels in the UK are rising and have undergone a sharp increase in the years since 1998

Figure 4 below shows the number of applications for asylum in the UK and how many of those were refused asylum, exceptional leave to remain (ELR), Humanitarian Protection (HP) or refused discretionary leave (DL).

Migrant workers

In 2004, 144,000 migrants came to the UK for work-related reasons. A survey conducted by the Chartered Institute of Personnel and Development (CIPD) in 2005 of over 1,200 UK organisations revealed that 27 per cent of employers surveyed were looking to recruit migrant workers with migrants from the new EU states as the most sought after. 18 per cent of employers look to recruit migrant workers because of their greater commitment and willingness to work. Migrants are mostly hired as a solution to long-standing recruitment difficulties; however, 5 per cent of employers hire migrant workers simply to cut wages.

Data collection

The Office for National Statistics derives its Total International Migration (TIM) figures from a variety of sources including Home Office data and the International Passenger Survey (IPS). The IPS is a voluntary sample survey that monitors inflow and outflow through all major points of departure between the UK and the rest of the world. It records data associated with country of visit/origin, purpose of visit, length of stay, age and gender, amongst other factors. The sample taken involves 250,000 interviews per year, representing 0.2 per cent of all travellers as they enter or leave the UK. The MN series from the Office for National Statistics are publications on international migration during the preceding ten years.

Policy development

Concern over the adequacy of UK immigration and asylum systems has led to recent developments in policy in recent years. These changes include a new asylum and immigration bill, processes for managed migration, establishment of a National Asylum Support Service (NASS) and developments in existing policies, such as those concerning migrant workers schemes and redefining the classifications of a refugee. *Updated 12 December 2006*

⇨ The above information is reprinted with kind permission from the Economic and Social Research Council. Visit www.esrc.ac.uk for more information or to view references for this article.

Migration in the UK – statistics

Figure 1: Total international migration 1996-2005

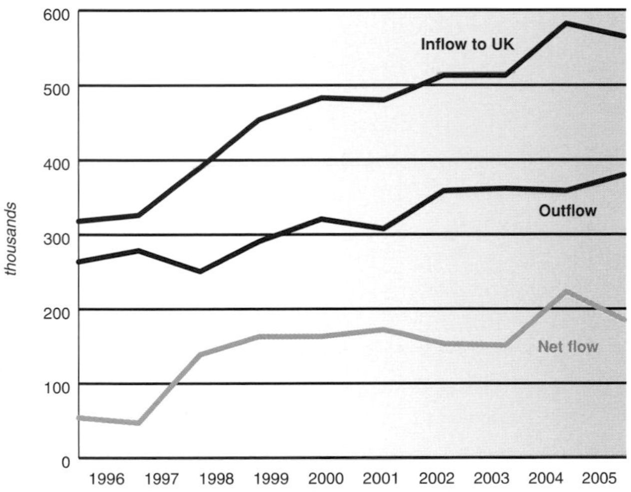

Source: Over 500 a day gained through migration to the UK *(2006), Office of National Statistics. Crown copyright.*

Figure 2: Origins of people granted settlement in the UK in 2004

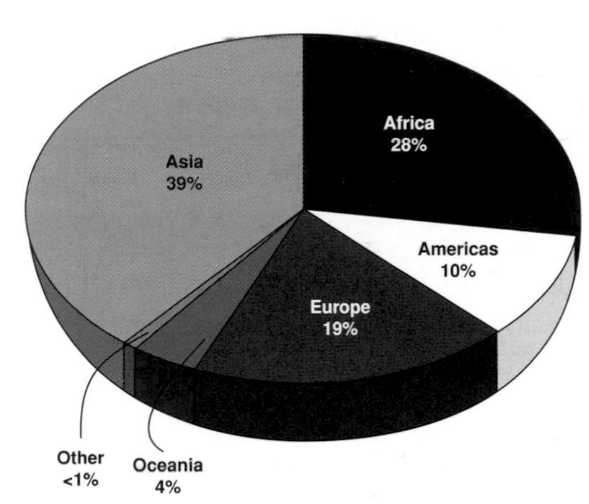

Source: Social Trends 36 *(2006), Office of National Statistics. Crown copyright.*

Figure 3: EU-15 asylum applications comparison 2005, including dependants

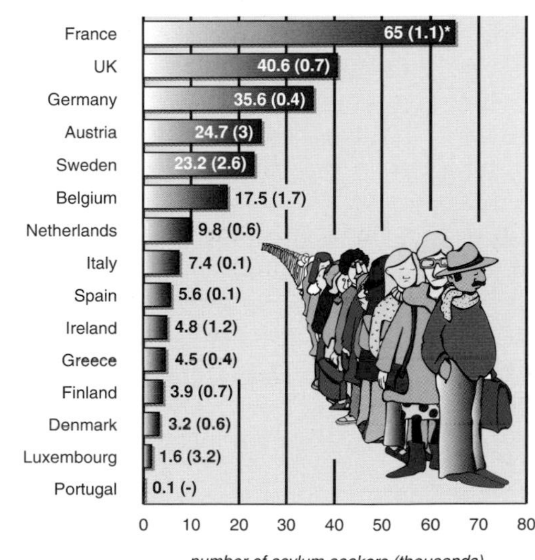

** Numbers in brackets indicate asylum seekers per 1,000 population*

Source: Social Trends 36 *(2006), Office of National Statistics. Crown copyright.*

Figure 4: Asylum applications granted 1997-2005

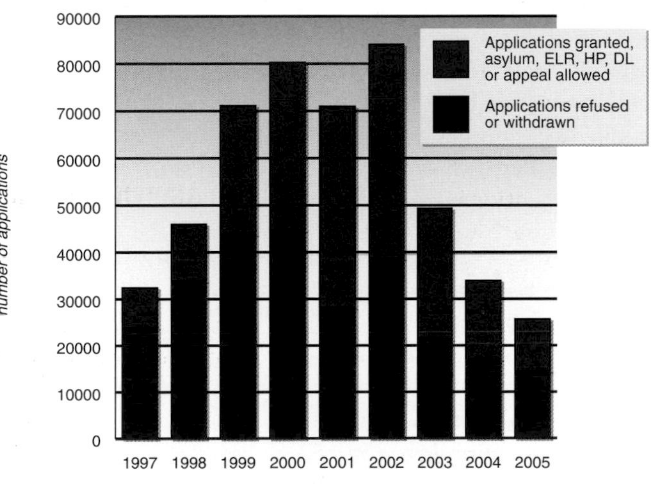

Source: Control of Immigration *(2005), Home Office and Office of National Statistics. Crown copyright.*

Statistics taken from the ESRC factsheet Migration in the UK. *© Economic and Social Research Council*

Migration from Bulgaria and Romania

Lessons from the most recent enlargement

On 22 July 2006 the Home Office released figures showing that 427,000 people from new EU member states have registered to work in the UK since May 2004. The figures also show that benefit claims by people from the new member states are increasing rapidly. While there had been 6,853 successful benefit claims made by workers from new member states this time last year, there have now been 42,057 successful claims. The figures shed light on the current debate about how to handle migration from Bulgaria and Romania when they join the EU (expected to be from the start of 2007).

A new briefing note released by Open Europe today argues that the UK *should* allow free movement of workers from Bulgaria and Romania – but that the UK must repeal the EU legislation which limits the Government's ability to control the movement of criminals and the rights of non-workers to access benefits.

We project that if the current policies remain in place then the UK should expect around 450,000 people from Romania and around 170,000 people from Bulgaria to come to the UK to work over the first two years after their accession. Making a success of such a large movement of people will require a new and better system than the Government's current Worker Registration Scheme (WRS).

Briefing: key points

The Home Office does not have accurate figures for the number of migrants in the UK.

The Government's current Worker Registration Scheme (WRS) is flawed. It fails to monitor the total number of people in the country, or the total number of new migrants claiming benefits. This is because it is expensive for workers and businesses to register, which encourages migrants to operate in the grey economy. Its main purpose is to act as a statistical reference for the number of migrants to the UK, but it does not capture: (a) the numbers of self-employed workers, (b) posted workers or (c) dependants and non-workers that have migrated. People who have been in the UK for more than a year are no longer required to register in the WRS.

Because workers are charged £70 to register with the WRS, and have to send away their passport, it encourages migrants to operate in the grey economy. The chair of the Commons Home Affairs select Committee John Denham has suggested that 'The number of people at the local level is often estimated at between two or three times the number the Government thinks are on the Worker Registration Scheme.'

Various other measures suggest the total number of people in the UK is higher than suggested by the WRS. In particular, figures from the ONS International Passenger Survey show that since EU enlargement over 4.5 million citizens from the accession countries have visited the UK. In the equivalent period of time going back to January 2002 there were 1.4 million visitors to the UK from the accession countries. This increase of 3.1 million visitors does not seem compatible with an increase of just 427,000 workers.

Research conducted for Defra and the Home Office in 2004 showed that labour providers are supplying over 100,000 accession state workers a year to agriculture and food processing. But in the first year of the WRS only 29,970 workers registered to work in agriculture and 11,385 in food processing, suggesting nearly 60,000 workers (or 60% within this industry) are 'missing'.

Failure to restrict access to benefits

In 2004 the then Home Secretary David Blunkett promised that: 'we will require accession nationals to be able to support themselves. If they are unable to do so, they will lose any right of residence and will have to return to their own country... If people want to come and work in Britain openly and legally, that is right. If they want to come and claim our benefits, that is wrong.'

However, in reality the WRS has failed to restrict access to benefits for migrant workers. There have now been 42,057 successful benefit claims by workers from the accession states. It is important to stress that these are only the claims made by those individuals who are on the WRS, and does not cover those who are not on it or no longer on it.

Outlook for Bulgaria and Romania

Managing migration from Bulgaria and Romania will be more challenging than the previous round of accessions to the EU. Research by the Home Office has found that during the recent round of accessions to the EU the proportion of people coming to the UK from each new member has been very strongly linked with the income level of their home country. Romania and Bulgaria have substantially lower incomes than any of the previous entrants.

Incomes in the countries which joined in 2004 varied between 72% of the UK average (in Cyprus) and 40% (in Latvia). Overall, the average was 54% of UK income per head. In Romania and Bulgaria incomes per head are 30% and 28% of the UK average respectively. If the strong relationship between home country income and numbers arriving in the UK continues to hold, and the same policy is applied as for workers from countries which recently joined the EU, we should expect around 450,000 people from Romania and 170,000 people from Bulgaria to register for legal work over the first two years of their membership of the EU.

However, because our projection is based on the WRS, it is worth stressing that this is not the same as the total number of people who will be in the country at any given time. On the one hand it does not measure non-registered workers and on the other it does not measure those who come for a short period and then leave.

Quotas for legal work may not be the answer

In the light of concerns about Bulgaria and Romania's accession there has been discussion about introducing quotas for the number of people from those countries who could legally work in the UK. Such controls are sometimes misrepresented as controls on the number of people coming to the UK. However, this is misleading.

EU legislation means that once Bulgaria and Romania join the EU, the UK will have to abandon its visa requirements from those countries anyway. People from both countries will also get an automatic three-month EU 'right to reside' – so even if the Government limits their right to work in the UK many will still be able to come to Britain. The experience of countries with such 'controls' suggests that many will then work in the grey economy. This means that they will still be able to access public services such as the NHS, but will not pay tax and indeed are more likely to be employed at illegally low wage rates, increasing downward pressure on the wages of low paid workers.

Quotas could also be legitimately circumvented by a number of legal routes under EU legislation. Under the EU's 1996 'Posted Workers Directive' Bulgarian and Romanian companies would still be able to post workers to the UK, and Bulgarians and Romanians would still be able to set up companies and come here as self-employed workers, under the EU's freedom to provide services.

Quotas for legal work could potentially lead to the worst of all worlds. Migrants who genuinely come to seek work legally, pay tax and contribute to society would be turned away, while criminals and those who come with no intention of working would still be let in. This could lead to substantial abuse of the UK's welfare system, but without providing any real economic benefit to Britain.

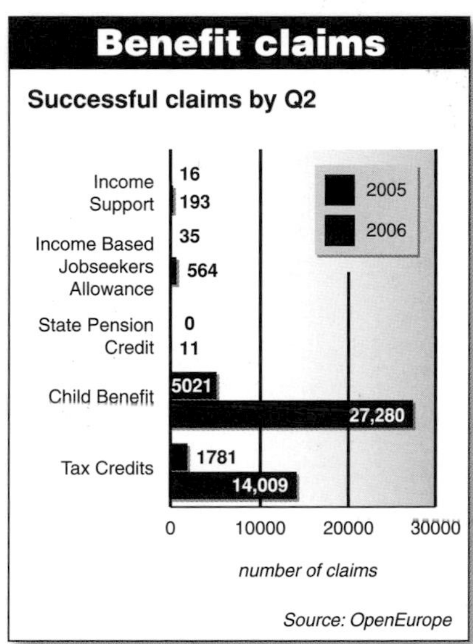

The solution is to allow free movement of workers – but repeal the EU legislation which makes it more difficult to control the movement of criminals and the rights of non-workers to access benefits. Overall, in order to manage migration from Bulgaria and Romania the Government should make four key changes to the current system as a priority:

- Repeal EU legislation which prevents criminals from elsewhere in the EU from being automatically deported. An EU directive agreed by the Government in 2004, which came into force in May this year (the Free Movement directive) means that the UK will not be able to automatically deport those who come to the UK and commit crimes.
- Introduce 'World Cup' style arrangements with Bulgarian and Romanian police to share information and ban known criminals from coming to the UK. At present there are no restrictions on criminals coming to the UK. In return for allowing free movement of people the Government should make deals with Bulgaria and Romania which will stipulate that the countries have a duty to inform the UK Immigration Service if known criminals are travelling to the UK.
- Tighten access to welfare to avoid legal problems later. The WRS limits migrants' access to welfare: but only to some types of benefits and then only for their first year in the UK. Stricter limits on access to welfare and for a longer period are going to be necessary if migration from Romania and Bulgaria is to be a success. Another reason to repeal the 2004 Free Movement directive is that it expands access to welfare benefits for non-workers from other member states. Indeed, the Government is said to be worried that the current restrictions could be challenged as a result. A Home Office memo leaked to the *Mail on Sunday* warned that the legal basis for the current restrictions 'is precarious and there is a strong risk of a successful challenge. This is a concern.' Earlier in the year the Government had to pass emergency legislation after losing a court case about access to council housing. The Government should tighten controls now to avoid legal problems later.
- Count people in and out – re-introduce embarkation controls. Rather than focus on monitoring a small section of those who have entered the UK, the Government needs to get a fuller picture. One simple and effective way would be to immediately introduce embarkation controls at all British ports and airports. This would enable the authorities to count the numbers entering and leaving the country. The Government has announced that it wants to introduce electronic embarkation controls – but only by 2014.

22 August 2006

- The above information is reprinted with kind permission from Open Europe. Visit www.openeurope.org.uk for more information.

Migration facts and figures

Information from the Trades Union Congress

Surveys define immigration in different ways, and official statistics do not usually include undocumented migrants. It is important to be careful about using the right statistics for different discussions. Trade unions' main concerns are about the world of work, so the figures in this section are for people born outside the UK, who are now living and working here, taken from an important recent article in *Labour Market Trends*. It would be confusing at this point to include statistics that include non-working dependants of migrants – but it is worth noting that the studies we quote for the impact of migration on social security, public services and housing do define migrants in this way.

In 2005 there were 1.505 million foreign migrants working in the UK, accounting for 5.4% of all employees. In the past ten years the number of migrant workers has increased by about 600,000. This is a phenomenon being seen across Europe. A study for the OECD, looking at migration between 1994 and 2001 found that 'the ratio of immigrants (no matter how defined) has grown steadily in all Western European countries considered, except Belgium'.

Nearly two-thirds of migrant workers in this country live in the South East of England – 45.3% live in London and another 18.5% in the rest of the South East. This preponderance has, however, become a little less noticeable recently: in the 1990s about 45% of new immigrants settled in London, but in 2002-5 this fell to 40%.

Immigrants are, on average, younger than the native-born population: 38.4 years compared with 39.9 years; 90% are aged between 15 and 44 (figures for all immigrants, not just those in employment).

Migrant workers tend to be more likely than UK nationals to work at either end of the spectrum – in professional or routine jobs – and less likely to work in intermediate jobs.

These differences are real, though less extreme than some reports have suggested. However, this pattern may be changing: the differences from UK nationals are increasing – recently arrived migrant workers are less likely to work in professional occupations and much more likely to work in routine jobs. This is illustrated by the data for people who were living outside the UK a year before the survey.

It is very likely that this change is connected to the entry of the East European states to the European Union in 2004, but it is far too early to tell whether it is a new trend or a shorter-lived phenomenon. This shift towards routine occupations has taken place despite the fact that migrants continue to be better educated than native workers. A study for the Bank of England looked at the age when people left full-time education, producing figures for those who were UK-born, immigrants and

Migration and employment

People living and working in the UK by socio-economic classification, 2005

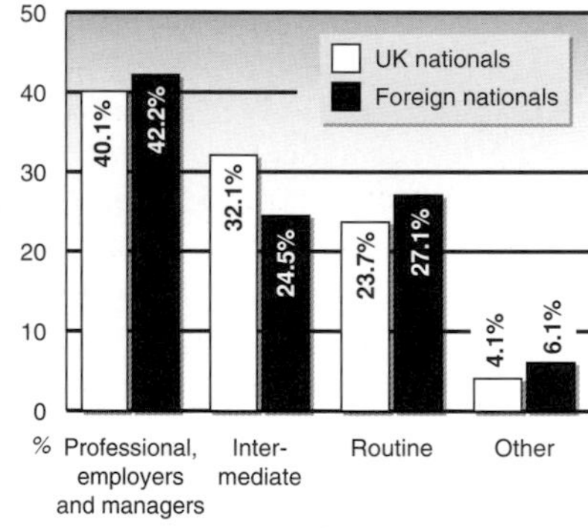

Source: Foreign Labour in the United Kingdom: current patterns and trends, *John Salt and Jane Millar, Labour Market Trends, ONS, Oct 06, pp 335 - 355, table 4*

Foreign nationals living and working in the UK now but outside the UK one year previously, by socio-economic classification, 2005

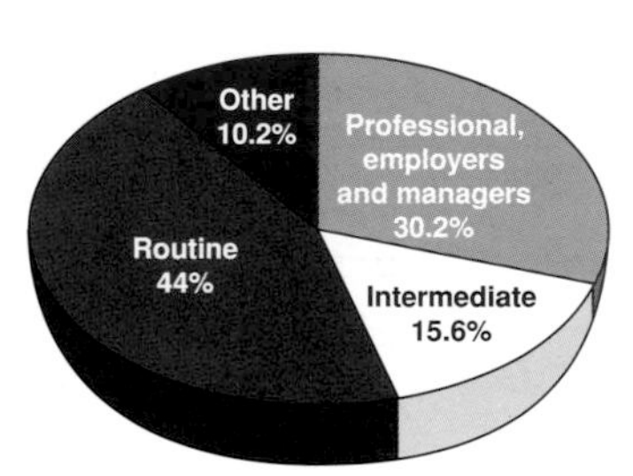

Source: Foreign Labour in the United Kingdom: current patterns and trends, *John Salt and Jane Millar, Labour Market Trends, ONS, Oct 06, pp 335 - 355, table 6*

Age at which immigrants and native-born people left full-time education, 2005

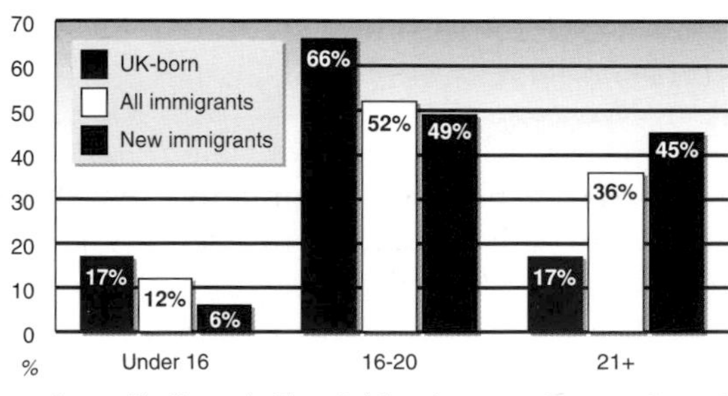

Source: The Economic Characteristics of Immigrants and their Impact on Supply, *J Salaheen and C Shadforth, Quarterly Bulletin, Bank of England, 2006 Q4, table B*

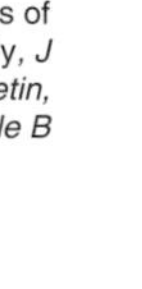

Proportion of workers earning below £5 an hour, 2005

UK born	All immigrants	New immigrants
10%	9%	16%

Source: The Economic Characteristics of Immigrants and their Impact on Supply, *J Salaheen and C Shadforth, Quarterly Bulletin, Bank of England, 2006 Q4, table B*

new immigrants (those who entered the UK during the survey year or the calendar year before the survey was carried out).

These figures are for all immigrants, and so include people who have come to the UK to study, but the Bank of England paper finds a similar occupational breakdown to the *Labour Market Trends* article used elsewhere in this section. In addition, the Bank finds that 'average hourly pay of "new" immigrants was not very different to existing immigrants through the 1990s, but since 2002, the real wages of "new" immigrants have fallen relative to the real wages of those born in the United Kingdom'. This is partly because, as noted above, more new immigrants are settling outside London, and partly because they are more likely to enter low paid jobs.

The migrant workers in the statistics in this section are mainly documented workers; it is very difficult for official statistics to catch up with undocumented migrant workers. The Home Office has estimated that there were 430,000 'unauthorised' migrants in the UK in 2001, and the Institute for Public Policy Research has concluded that 'while regular migrants to the UK come to fill vacancies across the skills spectrum, most irregular migrants are likely to be doing jobs that could be characterised as dirty, difficult and dangerous'. The IPPR has calculated that regularising the position of these workers would not only make it much more difficult for them to be exploited, it could produce as much as £1 billion extra a year in National Insurance contributions and income tax.

June 2007

⇨ The above information is reprinted with kind permission from the Trades Union Congress. Visit www.tuc.org.uk for more information or to view references.

Has migration led to unemployment?

Information from the Trades Union Congress

'East Europe migrants help take jobless to six-year high'
(Headline in the *Daily Mail*, 17 August 2006)

Linking immigration to unemployment is an old story; is it justified? Sometimes this link reflects what is known as the 'lump of labour fallacy'. This is the notion that there is a fixed amount of work that can be done in the economy and that if one group gets more of that work then existing workers will get less. However, the idea produces a rare example of agreement among economists, who nearly all believe that a key influence on the amount of work available is the level of demand in the economy – how much people are able to buy.

A thought-experiment can illustrate this: when the baby-boom generation reached working age the number of people entering the labour market far exceeded the number leaving it. This effect was a bit like a new wave of migrants arriving every year for over a decade. If immigration is a threat to jobs, then the baby boomers should also have been taking jobs away from existing workers and threatening higher unemployment. Not only did this not happen, we saw a great expansion of employment, because the new young generation increased the level of demand.

As Richard Layard has pointed out, across Western Europe, the USA and Japan in the last 40 years of the 20th century there was a very close relationship between the growth of the labour force (the number of people available to fill jobs) and the growth of employment (the number actually in jobs). This relationship has to be seen in the long term, as it is obscured by changes caused by the economic cycle, but, as Layard has also pointed out, those countries that responded to unemployment in the 1980s and 1990s by encouraging people to retire early or leave the labour market in some other way did *not* necessarily see their unemployment fall – there is no clear relationship between a country's change in labour force participation and its change in unemployment.

The empirical evidence backs up this theory. In 2003 a Home Office-sponsored study summarised US and European research: 'the common conclusion of this work, apart from a small number of exceptions, is that immigration has only very small or no effect on employment ... of workers already resident'.

2006 research for the Department for Work and Pensions found 'no discernible statistical evidence to suggest that A8 migration has been a contributor to the rise in claimant unemployment in the UK'. Treating the arrival of the A8 workers after 2004 as a 'natural experiment', the authors argued that, if these migrants were responsible for the increase in unemployment in 2005-6, then those districts where Worker Registration Scheme registrations had been concentrated should have seen the largest increases in unemployment. They found that there was a very slight correlation, but it was not statistically significant. In America similar studies have been criticised because immigrants might be expected to go to those parts of the country where they know there is a plentiful supply of jobs. The authors controlled for this by checking whether A8 registrations were more likely to be in districts that had had the highest employment rates in April 2004. In fact, A8 migrants were somewhat more likely to register in districts that had had a higher *un*employment rate just before accession.

In a similar vein Rebecca Riley and Martin Weale have noted that 'a broad view of the data does not suggest a clear general link between immigration and unemployment'. Net immigration has been rising since 1997, but the unemployment rate fell between January 1998 and August 2005, from 6.4 per cent to 4.7 per cent.

They also find that 'immigration since 1998 has raised GDP by 3.1 per cent. The immigration in 2004-5 has on its own contributed 1 per cent to GDP and, of this, the inflow from the new member states accounts for 0.2 per cent of GDP. Since the actual growth rates in 2004 and 2005 were 3.3 per cent and 1.9 per cent, it is obvious that the effect of immigration economic growth has been substantial.' The Treasury sees inward migration as accounting for 10-15 per cent of forecast trend economic growth.

None of this is to say that any *individual's* job is going to be unaffected by migration. Overall the impact of migration will be to increase employment for native workers, but as we see below, some employers are clearly recruiting migrant workers in preference to British workers. As the Treasury has noted in a discussion about changes in the structure of employment more generally, 'The process of redeployment inevitably brings transitional costs, which may fall particularly heavily on those least well equipped to cope with change – for example those with non-transferable skills. But the outcome for the economy on a whole is clearly positive; and there is a great deal governments can do to minimise transitional disruption to individuals' lives.'

Riley and Weale believe that A8 immigration has affected employment rates for less skilled workers, and we know that migrant workers are definitely on employers' minds. The Bank of England's business contacts have been telling the Bank that 'the availability of immigrant labour has been rising in the United Kingdom'. The Chartered Institute for Personnel and Development has been reporting for some time that migrant labour is popular with employers; in their 2006 recruitment survey they noted that 15% of organisations had targeted East European migrants, and another 12% intended filling vacancies from foreign countries more generally. The survey showed just under half of employers believing that this approach was successful in dealing with recruitment difficulties.

In 2005, CIPD controversially reported that employers are rejecting the 'core jobless' and would prefer to recruit migrant workers. Sizable minorities excluded hard-to-help groups such as people with a history of mental illness, even when it was against the law. A majority of employers had no policy of targeting 'core unemployed' people for recruitment; among those who did, migrant workers were more likely to be targeted than long-term unemployed and people with mental health problems.

It seems clear that immigration does not threaten the jobs of British-born workers overall, but there can be transitional problems, and the most disadvantaged workers may be the most likely to be disadvantaged in this process. We also know from anecdotal accounts that in certain, specific sectors migration may be causing job losses. For example, there is growing evidence that this may be happening in the construction sector although we know of no survey work which has been conducted to verify this.

This suggests three policy responses for unions. Firstly, unions should press for effective enforcement of current minimum employment standards, and make sure that migrant workers actually benefit from their rights to the minimum wage, sick pay, paid holidays and social security contributions. Secondly, unions should make an extra effort to organise migrant workers, extending union rates and conditions of employment to a vulnerable group of workers and thus ensuring that native workers are not undercut. Thirdly, British society generally gains from migrants' impact on output and their net fiscal contribution; it is only fair that the bulk of any gains should be used to enhance social security and services for those workers who may lose out, especially through extra rights to training and higher social benefit rates. The Treasury has recognised the case for 'appropriate social protection instruments' to 'prevent the most severe effects' of 'short-term adjustment costs'. Unfortunately the Treasury confines its discussion of the social purpose of social protection to the prevention of absolute destitution – this is not a fair bargain, and the trade union movement will insist that an open economy can only be operated fairly if the gains are applied to enhancing the social wage.

June 2007

⇨ The above information is reprinted with kind permission from the Trades Union Congress. Visit www.tuc.org.uk for more information or to view references.

Frequently asked questions

Information from Migration Watch

Do migrants add to economic growth?

Yes but they also add to population.

In a recent parliamentary debate, a Home Office Minister gave an official estimate that 'migration has increased output by at least £4 billion and (accounts for) 10-15% of economic trend growth'. But the Government had failed to take into account the addition to population. In 2005 net immigration was 185,000 which, on a population of 60 million, is 0.31%. At the same time the Government's estimate of £4 billion on a Gross Domestic Product (GDP) of approximately £1,250 billion is 0.32%. The benefit in terms of GDP per head is therefore trivial – about 0.01% of GDP or just 4p per head per week – less than a Mars bar per month.

An exchange of skilled workers is to everybody's benefit but it is not a sufficient reason for net foreign immigration at the present level

As for the claim that migration accounts for 10-15% of trend growth, the result is the same. Trend growth is 2.5% so 10-15% of trend growth is 0.25% to 0.375% of GDP. The effect on GDP per head is therefore a small negative or positive amount.

Other recent studies in the UK, and studies carried out in other countries, point to the same conclusion – namely that immigration makes little difference to GDP per head.

What is wrong with a 'managed migration policy'?

Nothing. But, in reality, it is not managed. Work permits are almost entirely employer driven. About 2 million non-settlement visas are issued every year yet there are no checks on departure. David Blunkett, when he was Home Secretary, has admitted publicly that 'he hasn't a clue' who is in Britain. Three-quarters of asylum seekers remain in Britain even if they are refused. The Government must put in place the necessary tools to be able to manage migration – notably, embarkation checks and ID cards. Until then, 'managed migration' will remain merely a slogan.

Do we need immigration to boost our economy?

Major studies in Canada and the United States have concluded that the benefit of immigration to the economy as a whole is positive but very small. The impact on GDP per head is a small fraction of 1%. In Britain, congestion costs probably wipe that out since we are 12 times as crowded as the United States. It follows that the case for large-scale immigration is a matter for decision on political and social grounds. The economic case is at best neutral.

Can we do without skilled workers from overseas?

An exchange of skilled workers is to everybody's benefit but it is not a sufficient reason for net foreign immigration at the present level of nearly 300,000 a year. In the medium term it is essential that we train and re-train our own workforce. Immigration can never be a substitute for this.

Would London collapse without foreign workers?

No. The jobs being done by foreigners in London are being done by British people in the many parts of the country where there are few, if any, immigrants. What is happening is that Londoners are moving out of London as large numbers of immigrants arrive. In the 10 years from 1995 to 2004 there was a net inflow of 880,000 international migrants to London. During the same time period a net 726,000 people left London to live in other parts of the United Kingdom.

Don't we need foreigners to do the jobs that British people are unwilling to do?

No. The underlying issue is pay rates for the unskilled. At present, the difference between unskilled pay and benefits is so narrow that, for some, it is hardly worth working. That partly explains why we have 1.7 million unemployed and a further 2.7 million on incapacity benefit, one million of whom the Government wishes to move from welfare to work. These figures include 1.25 million young people who are not in education, employment or training.

Who will pick strawberries?

There is a need for seasonal labour in the agricultural sector. There is no reason why students and others should not come to Britain temporarily for this purpose. The problem with present arrangements is that there is no check on their departure. However, since the recent expansion of the EU, workers from Eastern Europe have supplied most of the labour necessary for this purpose. From 1 Jan 2007 20,000 Romanians and Bulgarians will be admitted for six-month periods to work in agriculture and food processing but there will be no means of ensuring their departure at the end of their contract.

Do we need immigration to fill 600,000 vacancies?

No. The Government made this claim 6 years ago. From 2001 to 2005 there was net immigration of nearly 900,000 yet there are still about 600,000 vacancies. The reason is that immigrants also create demand so the argument from labour shortages leads to an endless cycle of immigration.

Revised 2 January 2007

⇨ The above information is reprinted with kind permission from Migration Watch. Visit www.migrationwatchuk.com for more.

Police chief warns of migrant crime impact

A chief constable has demanded more staff for her force to help cope with the effect on crime of the rise in migrant workers. By Sally Peck and agencies

Julie Spence of Cambridgeshire Police said more officers were needed to cope with complex problems posed by an influx of migrant workers following the expansion of the European Union.

She warned it could take as much as three times longer for officers to deal with a crime involving a migrant worker.

The chief constable said immigrants often arrived with 'different standards' from those in the UK, most notably over issues such as carrying knives and drink-driving, which has seen a 17-fold rise in arrests of foreigners in a year.

Mrs Spence said crime investigations could now involve trips abroad to interview relatives, and steep bills for interpreters. Officers must now be equipped to deal with people who speak a range of close to 100 languages, she said.

There is also a problem with 'feuds' between foreign nationals being brought across to the UK, Mrs Spence told BBC Radio 4.

'We recently had a murder and it was a Lithuanian on Lithuanian and it could easily have happened in Lithuania.

'But it didn't, it happened in Wisbech, so one of my staff spent a lot of their time in Lithuania trying to get underneath what was actually happening with the crime and criminality, which brings costs that you wouldn't have had before, which means something else has to give.'

She said: 'While the economic benefits of growth are clear, we need to maintain the basic public services infrastructure which means increasing the number of officers we have.'

Introducing a report on the impact of migration on policing, Mrs Spence said the effect of immigration brought problems ranging from lack of familiarity with local traffic laws to a rise in prostitution, apparently driven by the influx of large numbers of single men.

Between 50,000 and 80,000 of eastern England's 2.8 million economically active people are migrant workers, contributing about £360m a year to the economy, according to research from the East of England Development Agency (EEDA).

Migrant workers are also increasingly falling victim to crimes. In 2004, a report by Norfolk County Council and Norfolk police said immigrants working in fields and factories in west Norfolk were often victims of extortion, racism and crime.

Nick Clegg, the Liberal Democrat home affairs spokesman, said: 'The way ministers fund local public services, including the police, makes it incredibly difficult for communities to cope with the rapid changes in population that can be caused by immigration.

'It takes years for the extra money to come through from the Government for areas with high immigration, so it is no wonder the police can find themselves struggling.'

Liam Byrne, a Home Office minister, said it was vital that the social impact of the influx of immigrants be considered.

He said: 'It's because we want to hear voices like Julie Spence's that I set up the Migration Impacts Forum, so public services can help shape our tough points system which is introduced in around 150 days' time.

'At present, people who seek to come to the UK permanently, or as highly skilled workers are required to speak English. As the Home Secretary has said, we will be looking at extending this requirement to those coming to the UK to do lesser and low skilled work as well.'

Home Office officials said police had 'benefited from a significant increase in resources over the last decade'.

They said spending on police services had risen by nearly £5 billion from £6.2 billion to £11 billion since 1997.

Gordon Brown's spokesman said: 'The Chief Constable has given her views but I think it's important that we keep this in context.

'If you look at what's happening to total crime in Cambridgeshire, it's been on a clear downward trend.'

21 September 2007

What about a welcome amid the warnings?

Despite expressions of alarm from Cambridgeshire police last week, the benefits of immigration far outweigh its supposed evils

By Mary Riddell

The CCTV film shows a brutal scene. In an English high street, a gang is punching and kicking a figure on the ground. The force of the blows makes the victim's head knock backwards against the concrete wall of Woolworths. Otherwise, he is motionless. That footage comes from Wisbech, the Cambridgeshire town at the heart of the latest furore over immigration.

This assault, though, did not fit the template of the county's chief constable, Julie Spence, who last week sketched a police force struggling to cope with an influx of knife-carrying, drink-driving, feuding European migrants. The victims were two young Polish men and the assailants 10 British youths described, at a recent court hearing, as behaving 'like a pack of animals bringing down prey'.

The beating was a rare event. So was the murder of one Lithuanian by another, cited by Spence as evidence of pressure on her officers. A local council official told me he could recall only one similar incident, in which a man was burnt to death in his car, apparently by a fellow incomer. Still, it's all extra work for Spence's staff, no matter who's attacking whom. She has attracted almost universal praise for daring, in her comments on migrants, to break one of society's great taboos.

Which taboo would that be? It does not extend to my part of north London, where foreign decorators are viewed by their British rivals with the mistrust extended to Conquistadors by the Aztec empire. Nor have social niceties silenced hardliners in my Fenland home town, not far from Wisbech. A sample of the political correctness supposedly paralysing society has included a soccer riot after Portugal beat England, an attack in which a Portuguese mother and her baby were burnt out of their rented home and the grumbling of a small but ominous mutterati.

On Spence's patch, MP Malcolm Moss announced his investigation in 2005 into concerns that Wisbech was becoming 'a ghetto town'. This inquiry (result unknown) appeared to be based on one resident's allegation that migrant workers crammed into rented houses were failing to meet Ideal Home benchmarks by neglecting their front gardens and hanging sheets instead of curtains at their windows.

Migrant-bashing is not society's final taboo. It is its last, and cherished, public prejudice. Far from never daring to speak its name, it is a pub and media staple on a par with the *Blue Peter* cat and Jose Mourinho's Chelsea pay-off. Spence and Moss give succour, however unwittingly, to nationalists and xenophobes, as well as nurturing citizens' groundless fears that Britain is being swamped by lawless migrants.

Britain's history is built on migrant labour and expertise

There could be no greater mangling of the truth. Crime in Cambridgeshire is falling: 683,000 migrants have applied to work in Britain from Eastern Europe since 2004, but the rate is slowing. In the second quarter of this year, applications fell to 50,000, which is 6,000 lower than the same period in 2006. All but 3 per cent are employed and 56 per cent say they plan to stay for under three months. With 380,000 people leaving the country each year, we may be exporting more human beings than we import.

This is an odd basis for a panic. But other immigration figures are notoriously imprecise and our borders badly managed. Liberal Democrat home affairs spokesman Nick Clegg proposes a conditional amnesty for 600,000 'illegal' immigrants, a plan that should be adopted by government as a prelude to a properly managed system of admitting a range of people and helping them adapt. In implying, instead, that undocumented workers are a drain on welfare and should all 'go home', Immigration Minister Liam Byrne lets prejudice fester against all non-Britons.

Britain's history is built on migrant labour and expertise. Irish harvesters, Dutch engineers and Gypsy travellers all left their mark on the Fens, but

it took the Eastern Europeans to transform agro-industries, boost the local economy by £360m and get Costa Coffees and New Looks into time-warped high streets.

Obviously, importing people to do jobs that locals won't touch brings problems. Schools are under pressure, because they have too little funding and too few resources. In Wisbech, fishermen are reported to be alarmed that 'irresponsible' people (i.e. migrants) are dumping rubbish and eating the pike and carp that, according to convention and law, must be thrown back.

Warning signs may be put up in Eastern European languages. The next step, presumably, is a visit from one of Spence's officers, bearing a thumbed phrasebook containing such opening gambits as: 'Pot sa vorbesc cu tine?' ('Can I have a word with you?' in Romanian). In addition, a police guide includes warnings, in 15 different languages, not to fondle people without their permission or to urinate and spit in public.

Behind such Pythonesque integration strategies lie wild distortions. Incomers, many highly qualified, get parodied as the Vilnius variant of Fred Flintstone, while their hosts get branded racists. But for every Briton shouting 'F**k you' at a Polish waiter, there is another deploring migrants being housed in garden sheds. On the day Spence fuelled the latest 'scandal', Fenland District Council published an excellent and hopeful migrant strategy which attracted no notice whatsoever.

No one doubts that a few incomers break the law. But the real villains are the gang masters paying slave wages for six-day weeks and the landlords getting £1,200 a month for a three-bedroomed house by stacking workers in every room. Obviously, high rents are bad news for local people. Even so, mistrust the view that outsiders don't understand the price being paid by local communities. The East of England, increasingly affluent and with virtually full employment, has been propelled into the 21st century by people existing in a Dickensian shadowland of sweatshop labour.

Immigration has been one of Britain's great triumphs. But, for no good reason, the welcome mat wears dangerously thin

Tomorrow, Channel 4 will screen Ken Loach's film, *It's a Free World* ..., about the exploitation of immigrants without papers. Don't take his word for it. Go to the Fens and you will meet legal visitors existing on church charity and treated in ways that shame a civilised country. In a world of shrinking distances, the barriers of geography have been replaced by those of fear and bias.

As a final insult, leading citizens and politicians have the gall to suggest we are somehow the victims of those so shamelessly exploited in our land. Such warped reality bears a high price as Britain moves towards an immigration points system and the rich world imposes a form of globalised apartheid to keep the poor world out. It is getting harder all the time for genuine refugees to claim asylum in a country that welcomed in the Huguenots and the Jews. The sour protectionism that greets EU workers bodes ominously for a future in which wars and natural disasters may swell the world's refugees to a billion by 2050.

Immigration has been one of Britain's great triumphs. But, for no good reason, the welcome mat wears dangerously thin. The myth of the feckless welfare sponger is countered by the stream of would-be Britons paying, on top of their taxes, £34 a go to sit (or resit) their settlement exam and £80 for a citizenship ceremony.

The spirit of Britishness Gordon Brown wants to formalise can only be distilled from the raw materials on offer, whether they be warmth, cohesion or a gang of Fenland youths slamming a Polish man's head into a shop wall. Intolerance wreaks far more damage on Britain than any minor inconvenience posed by incomers. There is no immigration scandal, nor any doomsday scenario of over-population. Bogus fears are incubating a greater crisis. We are witnessing the brutalisation of Britain and the severance of human bonds.

23 September 2007

Human rights of female migrants

Women make up half of all migrants but their contributions are often overlooked

Today, half of all international migrants – 95 million – are women and girls. Yet, despite substantial contributions to both their families at home and communities abroad, the needs of migrant women continue to be overlooked and ignored.

This year's State of World Population report, *A Passage to Hope: Women and International Migration*, examines the scope and breadth of female migration, the impact of the funds they send home to support families and communities, and their disproportionate vulnerability to trafficking, exploitation and abuse.

The report, produced and published every year by UNFPA, the United Nations Population Fund, reveals that although migrant women contribute billions of dollars in cash and services, policymakers continue to disregard both their contributions and their vulnerability – even though female migrants tend to send a much higher proportion of their lower earnings back home than their male counterparts.

'This report calls on governments and individuals to recognise and value the contributions of migrant women, and promote and respect their human rights,' says Thoraya Ahmed Obaid, UNFPA Executive Director. 'There is an urgent need for stronger cooperation between countries to make migration more safe and fair. And there is a dire need for greater action to address the lack of opportunities and human rights violations that lead many women to migrate in the first place.'

The launch of the State of World Population 2006 comes just a week before the High-Level Dialogue on International Migration and Development in New York. This meeting, which will take place at the United Nations from 14 to 15 September, is the first of its kind to bring together the world's governments to discuss the many challenges and benefits of migration. The timing could not be more critical, nor the issues explored in *A Passage to Hope: Women and International Migration* more complex and pressing.

A Passage to Hope shows that although female migration can enhance equality and offer women opportunities simply not available at home, it can also lead to terrible human rights violations – cases of migration gone bad.

Half of all international migrants – 95 million – are women and girls

The human rights violations of trafficked women are well documented. Restrictive immigration policies that limit opportunities to migrate safely and legally fuel the desperation that drives millions of women and girls to entrust their well-being and, in some cases, their very lives to unscrupulous traffickers who misrepresent themselves as legitimate labour recruiters. Today, human trafficking represents the third largest illicit trade after drugs and gun smuggling. Unlike both however, trafficking victims remain an ongoing source of 'revenue' to be exploited over and over again until they are too ill or too worn out to continue. Many die as a result of their servitude – either as a direct result of violence or from contracting the many diseases including HIV to which they are susceptible.

'Although awareness and action against trafficking is growing, there is an urgent need to do more to end this terrible crime and the impunity that goes with it,' says Ms Obaid. 'The report calls for greater cooperation between and within countries to bring traffickers to justice and to provide services and human rights protection for trafficking victims.'

Today, domestic work remains one of the largest sectors driving international female labour migration. Every year, millions of women migrate from Asia, Latin America and the Caribbean, and increasingly from Africa, to Europe and North America, the Gulf States and the industrialising nations of Asia. However, labour laws rarely protect domestic workers, nor do they permit them to organise. This leaves millions dependent on employers for their continued legal presence in the host country, in addition to housing, food, and wages. The isolated nature of domestic work, coupled with official neglect and a dearth of appropriate labour protections, can relegate domestic workers to virtual slavery.

Another manifestation of female migration is the massive outflow of nurses from the developing world to industrialised countries. Ageing populations, coupled with a shortage of nurses and doctors in host countries, are fuelling demand, while crumbling health systems and poverty in developing nations are driving supply. The yearly exodus of 20,000 highly qualified nurses and doctors from Africa is worsening an already grave situation for a region ravaged by HIV/AIDS, malaria and high numbers of maternal and child deaths. 'Now is the time for vision and leadership on behalf of women migrants,' says Ms Obaid. 'Labour, human rights protections and sound immigration policies can ensure that migration for women is a passage to hope as the title of this year's State of World Population report suggests.'

6 September 2006

⇨ Information from the United Nations Population Fund. Visit www.unfpa.org for more.

Outline of the immigration problem

Information from Migration Watch

Introduction

Asylum claims have fallen sharply but immigration has trebled under the present government; it is now about fifteen times as high as asylum.

The issue is not about existing immigrant communities. Many have contributed greatly.

The question is about scale and pace. How many more immigrants should be admitted to the UK and how rapidly can they be integrated?

In a recent opinion poll 76% said that they favoured an annual limit on immigration. Only 10% were opposed.

Scale

Immigration is now on an unprecedented scale. The Asians from East Africa who arrived in the mid 1970s amounted to 27,000. We are now taking more than 10 times that number every year. Indeed, net foreign immigration reached 292,000 in 2005 (of which just 11,000 was accounted for by the net rise in asylum claimants).

Much of the recent debate has concerned immigration from Eastern Europe. From 1 May 2004, when eight East European countries joined the EU, 510,000 applicants have registered under the Worker Registration Scheme, 63% from Poland. (Workers from Eastern Europe can only claim full welfare benefits after they have worked here for 12 months.) However, the self-employed are not required to register. A Home Office Minister (Mr McNulty) has estimated the total over two years at 600,000. It is not known how many have since returned home. About half of those registered say that their employment is temporary. If they have all returned, net immigration from Eastern Europe would be about 150,000 a year (compared to the government's prediction of a maximum of 13,000). The ONS estimate that net migration from the new EU members in 2005 was 65,000. This was based on the data collected from the International Passenger Survey. Anecdotal evidence would suggest that this estimate is too low. Migration from the new EU countries is, of course, in addition to immigration from the rest of the world.

According to government projections, immigration will result in an increase in the population of the UK of 6 million in the 27 years from 2004 that is 6 times the population of Birmingham. Immigration (immigrants and their descendants) will now account for 83% of future population growth in the UK. The population projections took account of increased migration resulting from the expansion of the EU but they assumed that total migration flows would rapidly decrease from 255,000 in 2004-5 to just 145,000 in 2007-8. So far there has been no sign of a decrease in immigration from the new EU countries and the accession of Bulgaria and Romania (and possibly other East and Southern European countries) will add to immigration pressures.

In a recent opinion poll 76% said that they favoured an annual limit on immigration

Even this number does not include illegal immigrants. About 50,000 illegal entrants are detected every year but nobody knows how many succeed in entering undetected.

Legal immigration at the present projected rate will lead to a requirement of about 1.5 million houses in the period 2003-2026. England is now nearly twice as crowded as Germany, four times as France and twelve times as the US.

Meanwhile, asylum has been allowed to become a back door to Britain. In recent years over 60% have been refused permission to stay here but only 1 in 4 of those who fail are ever removed.

At present there is no reason why immigration should come to an end.

The pressure on our borders continues. Demand for visas has risen by 33% in 5 years and is now 2.5 million per year. In 2003 one in five visa-issuing posts was consistently unable to cope with the daily demand for visas, despite the time allocated to each case being reduced to only eleven minutes. No one is recorded as they enter or leave the country.

Economic benefit?

The economic benefit from this inflow is very limited. Government arguments are fallacious. Immigration is not essential to our economic growth. It adds to economic growth but also adds nearly proportionately to our population so that the benefit to the host community is small. (A result found also in the US, Canada and Holland.) In the UK some results show a negative impact on GDP per head – others show a small positive impact equivalent to about 4p per head per week.

Immigrants will have little impact on our ability to pay pensions in future. The Turner Commission dismissed this argument for the simple reason that immigrants too will age and require pensions. Their financial input to the Exchequer is, despite government claims, approximately neutral.

Immigration is welcome to many employers because it holds down pay levels, especially for the unskilled, and contributes to lower interest rates. It can also be a source of cheap skilled labour with no training costs. But it is the taxpayer who picks up all the costs of the extra infrastructure required.

To the extent that immigration holds down wages it makes it more difficult for the government to achieve their stated aim of moving from welfare to work the 1.7 million unemployed and the 2.7 million on Incapacity Benefit. There are now 1.25 million young people under 25 in Britain who are not in work, in full-time education or training.

Are immigrants doing jobs the British will no longer do? No. In large parts of Britain where there are few, if any, immigrants, British people are doing all these jobs. The fundamental problem is the benefits trap. Wages are held down to a level where for some there is little benefit in working rather than collecting benefits. Wages should be allowed to rise to make lower paid jobs worthwhile and to encourage productivity. Increasing productivity is the only way that a nation can become richer.

Where is this leading?

There is growing resentment among the native population of whom 70-80% wish to see a tougher immigration policy. They feel that their concerns are being ignored, or dismissed; only 10% feel that the government is listening to public opinion on immigration. The ethnic population is also concerned about the direction of events. A majority of them (55%) also wish to see tighter immigration control. A majority of the population (69%) feel that Britain is losing its own culture.

The natural tendency of some immigrants to join their own communities, and to choose spouses from their countries of origin, is leading to the formation of parallel communities with little contact, or identification, with mainstream British culture. Indeed, in some cases the younger generation is growing up hostile to British culture.

There are also frictions between different communities, sometimes encouraged by satellite television from their home areas. E.g. Pakistani/Indian. Caribbean/Somali. Pakistani/Kurd.

The performance of different ethnic communities varies greatly. Some are very successful, such as the Chinese and Indians. Other communities are being left behind in the educational and employment stakes, notably Caribbeans, Pakistanis and Bangladeshis. Migrants are nearly twice as likely to be unemployed as the native population.

The impact is very substantial. Over the next twenty years, one in three new households will be down to immigration. Since brownfield sites provide two-thirds of new homes, net immigration is the main reason for greenfield development. The extra population also adds to the pressure on transport and water supplies, both of which are already facing serious difficulties.

Furthermore, there are significant movements within Britain. In the last ten years, 600,000 Londoners have left the city to be replaced by 700,000 immigrants. This is changing the whole nature of London and other major cities. This outflow of people is higher from boroughs with a high percentage of ethnic minorities.

The Chairman of the CRE has pointed out that whites will soon be in a minority in Leicester, Birmingham, Bradford and Oldham perhaps by 2016. He has also warned that we are sleepwalking towards segregation.

What should be done?

We should be clear about the facts, frank about the problems, and constructive about the solutions.

A major step must be to limit the scale and pace of further immigration as clearly implied by the government's own cohesion panel. They reported that the pace of change (for a variety of reasons) is simply too great in some areas at present. An annual limit is essential to restore public confidence in the system.

The introduction of such a limit would be a considerable task and would take some years to be made affective.

The ideal would be to achieve a position where the numbers of people entering Britain was similar to the number emigrating.

Thereafter we should encourage more explicit nation building so as to integrate the minorities we have. This should involve language teaching, skills training and assistance in finding employment.

Revised 2 January 2007

⇨ The above information is reprinted with kind permission from Migration Watch. Visit www.migrationwatchuk.com for more information.

Irrationality grips the British concerning migrants

Rapid migration is not a cost-free option, but the public must accept that without it parts of our economy would collapse

By Madeleine Bunting

Let's start with potatoes. Thousands of them will be scrubbed, peeled and land on the dinner plates of those in Bournemouth for the Labour party conference this week. They'll get eaten, barely noticed, as the business of politics runs at its usual hectic conference pace; there will be gossip, intrigue and earnest debate, but none will touch on the potatoes. The mountains of salad leaves, tomatoes and cucumbers will similarly prompt little comment, nor the freshly laundered sheets or the scrubbed baths of Bournemouth hotels. And so the list goes on in the thousands of details of life eased by Britain's migrant labour force.

When Gordon Brown gets up today, he will probably refer to his economic record of growth combined with low inflation and low unemployment, but what he is much less likely to acknowledge is the key role that hundreds of thousands of migrant workers have played. Instead of claiming it for himself as a feat of remarkable economic management, Brown could give credit where some of it is due – to an army of cheap labour that has subsidised our lifestyles, keeping prices of food and hotels down, buses running, streets swept and rubbish collected. Imagine Brown thanking, in his speech today, the Poles, Latvians and Lithuanians who have dug up his dinner and served it, or the hundreds of foreign-born doctors and nurses filling the gaps in the NHS. Dream on.

In a poll earlier this year, 47% of the British people insisted migration had been bad for the economy and 76% wanted stricter border controls

No, Brown is much too savvy a politician; he's been wary of going anywhere near this most difficult of public debates. Yet in a poll in the summer, voters put reducing immigration as the task they most wanted the new prime minister to tackle, well ahead of health or education. He may dodge the issue today, but at some point Brown has to get stuck into how you persuade the voters that: a) migrants bring economic benefits – indeed, parts of our economy would collapse without them; b) rapid migration is not a cost-free option; and c) it's worth paying for.

That's the three-point deal that accompanies your cheap potatoes to the plate, but it's a deal that is frequently misrepresented. Last week, with the intervention of the chief constable of Cambridgeshire police, the focus was on the pressure migrants put on public services; our news story today highlights how some British low-skilled workers can lose out. What gets much less attention is the raft of reports – PricewaterhouseCoopers, the Bank of England, the TUC – acknowledging the beneficial effects of migrant workers overall: they have not led to increased unemployment and have been a major contributor to economic growth.

Public opinion doggedly refuses to believe it. In a poll earlier this year, 47% of the British people insisted migration had been bad for the economy and 76% wanted stricter border controls. This is a peculiarly British response; the same poll found that Spain, which has also enjoyed strong economic growth and an influx of migrant workers, had nothing like the same suspicion.

A curious irrationality has gripped the British on this: you could characterise it as wanting our cheap potatoes, eating them and then insisting that we'd never liked or wanted them in the first place.

On most other complex issues the public get the right end of the stick, so why not migration? There are two factors that repeatedly send the debate off course. The first is that everyone – the government, the Bank of England, local authorities – acknowledges they don't have much of an idea about the numbers. Who's come, who's gone home again? Who is working where or for what wages? How many kids are arriving in schools? How many need a GP? Earlier this month, the Office for National Statistics threw up its hands; the census and the surveys on which it bases its data can't keep up with a highly mobile migrant population. The Labour Force Survey, which is the gold standard of statistical research on work in this country, only gathers data from those with a landline. It can't reach a mobile-phone generation of migrant workers.

Without accurate figures, alarmist myths cannot be convincingly squashed

Without accurate figures, alarmist myths cannot be convincingly squashed. If the inhabitants of Lincolnshire's Boston see a 10-15% increase in population from migrant workers, how do you convince the public that this is not an experience about to be unrolled across the country, but is specific to the needs of the local agricultural industries? Without accurate figures, public services cannot be effectively planned; there will be sudden, sharp squeezes in unexpected places – such as schools suddenly seeing an influx of pupils with English as a second language.

And this relates to the second factor that distorts the debate. The benefits of migrant labour are spread across the whole country – everyone's food is a little cheaper, interest rates have not gone up as much as they might – while the costs of migrant labour can bear disproportionately on particular communities. For the media, the former is not a story, the latter most definitely is. Rural areas with small populations are suddenly facing some very complex challenges: Boston, a small market town of 58,000 people, now has 30-40 languages. Migrant workers are very mobile and no sooner has one tranche learnt English and worked out the recycling (rubbish is one of the biggest complaints from their neighbours), they've moved on and the next lot have arrived. For a small local authority charged with promoting community cohesion, this is pretty daunting.

Finally, there is another aspect of the cost of migrant labour which gets far less attention than it deserves – those borne by the migrants themselves. As the Citizens' Advice Bureaux in both Boston and Bournemouth acknowledge, many of the migrant workers coming through their doors are being exploited. Sometimes they don't get the minimum wage, or there are unexplained deductions from their pay packet for accommodation or administration. There are also abuses of their hours. They get penalised or even sacked if they question their working conditions. There are plenty of Brits who make a handsome packet from such employment practices, as Ken Loach's film *It's a Free World* – broadcast tonight on Channel Four – disturbingly portrays.

Such employers can get away with it; it's estimated that an employer's chance of being inspected by the Health and Safety Executive is once every 12-20 years – once every 200 years for breaches of the minimum wage. Despite increases for enforcement announced at the TUC two weeks ago, we have a sham system of ensuring decent conditions for these migrants, as the TUC's commission on vulnerable employment is uncovering. Most of the regulation is in place (though the government's reluctance to sign up to the EU directive on agency workers is a glaring gap), but the onus is put on the migrants themselves to know how to bring a complaint. What they risk by doing so is considerable, so the status quo goes unchallenged.

In Bournemouth this week, Brown and his cabinet will be benefiting from the influx of Poles to the town. As they are handed their cups of tea, or crawl into their carefully made beds, one hopes their consciences might be stirred to challenge the double standards of British sentiment and reframe the public debate around how to manage migration's costs effectively and justly.

24 September 2007

Does migration hurt migrants?

Information from the Trades Union Congress

The World Bank recently modelled the potential economic gains by 2025 from increased migration. The baseline was a world in which the proportion of migrants in each region stays the same over time, and in the alternative scenario migration increases enough to produce a 3% growth in the size of the workforce in high-income countries. Across the world as a whole, the alternative scenario raises total income by $356 billion – a 0.63% increase. The biggest gainers are the migrant workers themselves, who are $162 billion better off: increased migration raises their income by 199%. Natives in the high-income countries and those who stay behind in the developing countries are slightly better off, but old migrants in the high-income countries are significantly worse off.

Although migrant workers are the clearest gainers from migration in terms of income there are severe costs as well. Migrant workers are often exploited, and can face severe deprivation – on average, their incomes are higher than they would

be in their home countries, but they often earn much less than native workers would for the same work, and they have to face British living costs. We know that the health of the most disadvantaged migrant workers is precarious, and that they face reduced psychological well-being in the event of unemployment, poverty and poor health or being a victim of crime/racial harassment.

An important study, based on interviews with 200 migrant workers, found that migrant workers are more likely to work in jobs with higher health and safety risks and to be even more at risk than other workers. More than a third of those surveyed had had no health and safety training, and a quarter had either had an accident or had witnessed a migrant co-worker having an accident.

The World Bank reports that, 'in general, emigration does impose hardships on family members left behind', though it also 'improves families' ability to make compensating adjustments that mitigate those hardships'. Being a member of a group that is a net gainer from migration is, however, no guarantee that an individual will actually feel well off – a recent study of East European migrants in Scotland reported increasing levels of homelessness. A large-scale research project, involving interviews with 600 migrant workers and 500 employers, found that:

- Migrant employees earned less than the average for all employees, and their average hours were longer.
- Migrants working as au pairs and in hospitality commonly worked unpaid overtime; those working in construction and agriculture were paid overtime, but not necessarily at a higher rate.
- Only a minority received benefits like paid holidays, sick leave and free accommodation.
- Workers who were 'illegally' resident often experienced vulnerability, fear and anxiety.

Another study, based on interviews with 124 employers, found that most of those interviewed said they employed migrants on the same terms and for the same pay as domestic workers, but there were 'many anecdotal reports of migrant workers receiving lower pay than domestic workers, experiencing long hours, poor conditions and few employee rights. Many of these reports related to the practices of labour providers and were concentrated in low-skill jobs.'

June 2007

Incomes of migrants

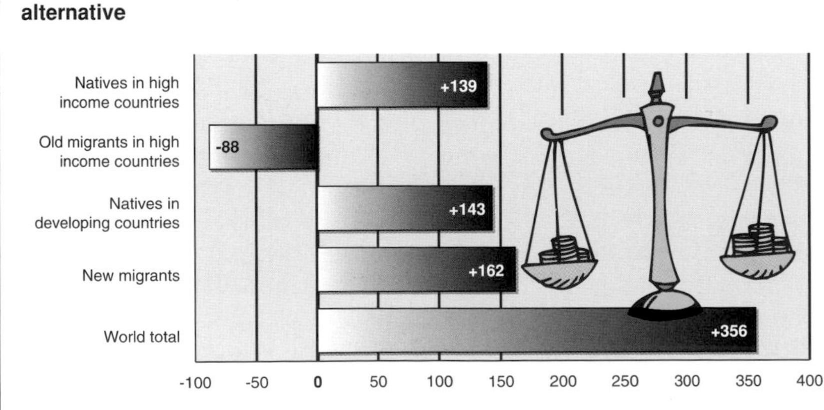

Source: Global Economic Prospects 2006: economic implications of remittances and migration, World Bank, 2006, table 2.3

- The above information is reprinted with kind permission from the Trades Union Congress. Visit www.tuc.org.uk for more information.

HIV, immigrants and immigration

Information from AVERT

Between 120 and 150 million people will remain for an extended stay outside their country of citizenship this year and most of us know someone who has relocated to a new country or area. But what exactly is migration? And who are migrants? What motivates people to leave their country of birth, how many are moving to the UK, and what problems are they bringing with them?

Theoretically, migration can be seen as a simple process that consists of three phases: where a person comes from, where they are going, and where they end up

What is migration?

Theoretically, migration can be seen as a simple process that consists of three phases: where a person comes from, where they are going, and where they end up. Migration is also about how a person travels; the length of time they are away; why they left in the first place; the relationships they maintain with home while they are away, and how far they are from home. Migration is often cyclical or seasonal, as people return home for periods of time.

When a person is deciding on whether to leave their country of origin a combination of 'push' and 'pull' factors determine where to go, how to go and for how long. Push factors, such as political unrest, war, persecution, famine, social upheaval, lack of opportunities and lack of infrastructure are what encourage people to leave. Pull factors, such as economic prosperity, political stability, professional opportunities and labour shortages are what encourage people to come to a country.

Who are migrants?

A migrant is someone who moves from one place or country to another. An emigrant is someone who leaves his or her own country to settle in another, and an immigrant is someone who comes as a resident to a new country. In terms of the UK, emigrants are people who leave the UK to live elsewhere, and immigrants are people who come from other countries to live in the UK.

'Migrants may be defined by their legal status or ethnicity... If we exclude short term visitors (tourists for example) the most important categories [for the UK] are labour migration, refugee migration, resettlement migration, internal migration and commuting.'

The UK tends to define immigrants in terms of the extent to which they mesh with the native culture, socially, ethnically and linguistically. However, it is a person's legal status which determines whether they are allowed to stay in the UK. If a person wishes to come to the UK for longer than a short visit there are only a limited number of legal avenues.

Migrants and sexual health

Being a migrant in itself is not a risk factor for sexual ill health. Indeed migrants (especially economic migrants) from many countries are more likely to be healthier, younger and more economically active than those who remain. There are, however, many factors that put migrants at a high risk of poor health in general.

Individual factors

Health beliefs

An individual's ethnic background or cultural heritage may exert a strong influence on their health belief systems and ultimately health-related behaviours. In the UK it is a widely held health belief that if a person goes outside with wet hair they will get a cold. People arriving here from other countries come with their own health beliefs.

Health-seeking behaviours

A person's health beliefs often have an impact on their health-seeking behaviour. Many migrants do not access health services unless they have symptoms of an illness. Additionally migrants, such as asylum seekers, may not feel entitled to access healthcare facilities in a new country, may be unaware of their entitlements or may have linguistic barriers.

High-risk behaviours

The majority of migrants travel alone. Being separated from family or regular partners, loneliness, depression, poverty and anonymity may cause a person to take risks they would not take at home. Misconceptions about host country norms and the pressure to 'fit in' may also lead to increased risk taking, both as regards sexual behaviour and drug use.

Exploitation

Migrants are often subject to exploitation and those who find themselves in need of money or services, may turn to selling or trading unprotected sex in order to survive.

Social and environmental factors

Socio-economic deprivation

Migrants who are fleeing poverty may well find themselves in similar situations when they arrive at their destination. As well as putting a person at risk of exploitation, problems such as poor housing and lack of food are likely to be far more pressing than poor sexual health. These factors may also push migrants into risky situations or behaviours (e.g. sex work).

Racism, xenophobia, discrimination, stigma or other disadvantage

Along with the stigma and discrimination that goes with having an STI, people may well have to cope with stigma and discrimination attached to migrants from particular regions. This often leads to a delay in seeking treatment resulting in poorer health outcomes.

The countries that migrants travel between must also be taken into consideration when assessing their risk of having sexually transmitted infections. People from countries with a high HIV prevalence may emigrate to countries where there is a low HIV prevalence, or vice versa. An immigrant from a high prevalence country is more likely to have HIV than one from a low prevalence country.

HIV/AIDS in Britain's migrant populations

Information on HIV/AIDS and migrants comes from a number of sources. One of these is the Health Protection Agency, which analyses and disseminates data on HIV trends in the UK. Although no data is collected about the legal status of people with HIV, some information is collected about the proportion of infections acquired overseas and the distribution of HIV infection across Britain's ethnic minority communities. For people born outside the UK, data are collected about their country of origin and date of arrival in the UK.

Migration and HIV: the response in the UK

Over the last few years many stories have appeared in the press about the burden migrants with HIV have placed on the National Health Service (NHS). Misinformation about asylum seekers and illegal immigrants has lead to discrimination and stigmatisation of many migrant groups. Stories about 'treatment tourism', suggesting people are coming to the UK purely for free treatment, have led to calls for the mandatory HIV testing of visitors to the UK. From a public heath point of view, according to the United Nations:

'there is no public health rationale for restricting liberty of movement or choice of residence on the grounds of HIV status… any restrictions on these rights based on suspected or real HIV status alone, including HIV screening of international travellers, are discriminatory and cannot be justified by public health concerns.'

With regard to the burden migrants place on the health system, HIV treatment represents less than 0.1% of the total NHS budget. The NHS spends £3.8 billion per year on alcohol-related illnesses as opposed to £279 million on HIV treatment and prevention. Indeed the NHS expenditure on heart disease is £7 billion a year.

Current legislation

In April 2004, in an effort to prevent 'treatment tourism', the Government introduced controversial changes to regulations concerning HIV treatment for overseas visitors to the UK. Previously, NHS treatment for all conditions was free for anyone who had lived in the UK for at least 12 months, as well as anyone applying for asylum or the right to remain in the country. This allowed the majority of overseas visitors who required HIV medication to obtain it without charge. The new changes dictate that only those residing in the UK legally have access to HIV treatment without charge. This means that failed asylum seekers, illegal immigrants and those residing in the country 'without proper authority' are now excluded from free treatment.

The Government argues that:

'The only people who have anything to fear from [the] change are those who are abusing the system and shouldn't be here.'

Yet a number of organisations have argued that the legislation is inhumane and unethical, since the groups affected are among the most vulnerable to HIV in the UK, are too poor to be able to pay for treatment, and often cannot leave the country for fear of persecution – effectively they are stranded without help.

Who is allowed to stay in the UK?

People from EU countries are allowed to stay in the UK for as long as they like. People from non-EU countries must fit into one of several legal categories, and must satisfy certain criteria if they are to be permitted to enter and remain in the UK. The criteria they must satisfy varies depending on their country of origin, and the amount of time they are permitted to remain in the UK depends upon which legal category they are in.

An individual's ethnic background or cultural heritage may exert a strong influence on their health belief systems and ultimately health-related behaviours

Asylum seekers

All countries are subject to the 1951 UN Convention Relating to the Status of Refugees or its 1967 Protocol Convention. Under these rules, countries must grant refuge on humanitarian grounds to people who flee a country owing to 'a well-founded fear of persecution' for political, ethnic or religious reasons.

A person applying for sanctuary in a country under these rules is an 'asylum seeker'; if their application is accepted they become a 'refugee'. During 2004, there were 676,000 first instance or appeal applications for asylum or refugee status submitted to governments or UNHCR offices in 143 countries. The number of applications from individuals seeking asylum in the UK fell by 33% between 2003 and 2004, from 49,305 to 33,960. The main countries from which applications came were Iran (3,455), Somalia (2,585), China (2,365), Zimbabwe (2,065) and Pakistan (1,710).

Students

University students are allowed to enter, but if it is thought they will stay after their course has ended they may be denied entry. In 2004, 294,000 students were permitted entry to the UK, and 146,555 were granted extensions of leave to remain in the country.

People wishing to work in the UK

The Work Permit System is a scheme which allows employers to transfer or recruit skilled people from non-European Union (EU) countries. The employer applies for a work permit for a named individual for a maximum of five years. In 2004 121,235 work permits were issued in the UK. Permit holders are allowed to apply for permanent settlement after the permit runs out, a course of action which has grown increasingly popular in recent years, with numbers rising from 4,335 in 2001 to 16,170 in 2004.

Other work-related categories include: the working holidaymaker scheme where individuals aged 17-27 from commonwealth countries are allowed to take non-professional jobs as part of their holiday (e.g. working in bars and restaurants); approximately 15,000 people were allowed to enter the UK to work under the Seasonal Agricultural Workers Scheme and Commonwealth Citizens with a UK-born grandparent who are allowed to seek employment.

Family members

Those who are settled in the UK can bring dependent members of their family to the UK. In 2004, approximately 34,230 family members joined British citizens or persons previously granted settlement.

Updated 17 July 2007

⇨ The above information is reprinted with kind permission from AVERT. Visit www.avert.org for more information or to view references for this article.

Improving population statistics

Information from the Office for National Statistics

It is increasingly important to have high quality statistics on migration and the population, for policy development and for planning and providing public services. Achieving this aim is challenging in the context of increasingly complex lifestyles and changes in migration to and from the UK over the last decade.

It has long been recognised that international migration is one of the most difficult components of population change to measure accurately. Large numbers of people travel into and out of the UK every year although migration numbers can be very different between one part of the country and another. There is no single, comprehensive source which can provide the information, at national and local levels, that is required for statistical purposes.

It is in the context of these pressures that the work of improving migration and population statistics has been prioritised. It is focused on making improvements to the methods and data sources used to estimate the population at national and local levels during the inter-censal period. These improvements are needed to minimise the risk of divergence between the rolled forward mid-year population estimates and the 2011 Census-based population estimates, and to better understand the differences that remain.

Revised 26 October 2007

⇨ Information from the Office for National Statistics. Visit www.statistics.gov.uk for more.

Brits abroad

Mapping the scale and nature of British emigration. Summary of a report from the Institute for Public Policy Research

While immigration into the UK has received intense academic, media and political attention in recent years, the other side of the migration equation – namely emigration – has received relatively little consideration. This report aims to help address this situation by presenting fresh evidence and analysis of the scale and nature of contemporary British emigration.

Our research suggests that around 5.5 million British nationals live overseas permanently (equivalent to 9.2 per cent of the UK's population)

While Britons have been moving all around the world for centuries, the scale of emigration from the UK in recent years has been staggering. Over the 39 years between 1966 and 2005, the UK experienced a total net loss of some 2.7 million British nationals. In other words, every year for the past 39 years, around 67,500 more British nationals left the UK than came back to it. Over the last decade, while the dominant story has been one of rising immigration of non-British nationals, relatively little attention has been paid to rising net emigration among British nationals. In 2005, for example, 198,000 Britons left to start new lives abroad, while 91,000 came back to the UK.

Our research suggests that around 5.5 million British nationals live overseas permanently (equivalent to 9.2 per cent of the UK's population). In addition, an estimated 500,000 British people live abroad for part of the year, mainly through second-home ownership. This means that nearly one in ten British nationals lives part or all of the year abroad. It also means that there are more Britons living abroad than there are foreigners living in the UK. When those claiming British ancestry are added, the figure climbs to around 58 million. In terms of absolute size and geographical spread (of both British nationals and those claiming ancestry), it is likely that only the Indian and Chinese diasporas rival Britons living abroad.

Britons who live abroad are spread across the globe. While around three-quarters of all Britons living abroad live in the top 10 destination countries (Australia, Spain, US, Canada, Ireland, New Zealand, South Africa, France, Germany and Cyprus), some 112 countries are estimated to have a British population of more than 1,000.

Britons living abroad are not a homogenous group. They hail from different demographic and socio-economic backgrounds, and have moved at different times to different countries for different reasons. For most of the last two centuries, the most popular destinations for British people emigrating were the old settler colonies of Australia, Canada, New Zealand and South Africa. Today, Australia and New Zealand remain popular destinations, though the so-called 'Ten Pound Poms', who went as part of an Australian government scheme to encourage emigration to Australia, have given way to skilled professional emigrants. European countries are also becoming increasingly popular destinations, as cheap travel and European Union (EU) integration make countries such as Spain, France and Portugal more accessible to British emigrants.

The UK is at the crossroads of the global movement of skilled people. During the second half of the twentieth century, British emigrants became increasingly skilled. Two-thirds of all Britons who leave the UK do so to seek employment abroad, and are replaced by skilled professionals from elsewhere in the world.

There has been significant growth in the number of British emigrants who are retiring or taking early retirement abroad. The UK government is currently estimated to be paying more than £2 billion per annum in pension payments to more than one million UK state pensioners living overseas. It is also transferring several hundred million pounds per annum to help other EU states provide healthcare to UK pensioners living in Europe.

Our research reveals that the dominant motivations for emigration seem to be positive attributes of the places emigrants would like to go to rather than the negative attributes of the UK. Contrary to some claims, only a minority of people (12 per cent) say they would like to leave because they do not like what Britain is becoming. We have classified the main motivations for why people emigrate into four 'flow' factors:

- Family ties – people moving to be with a partner or returning to their country of origin after spending many years in the UK.
- Lifestyle – working-age families and retirees attracted by a better quality of life, better climate, better value for money and better recreational options abroad.
- Overseas adventure – primarily young adults spending a short period abroad looking to gain new experiences and skills, some of which may help them with their career when they return.
- Work – workers, usually skilled, lured by career opportunities abroad.

The majority of British expatriates slip easily into their new communities. However, a small but significant minority are finding the settlement experience much more challenging. Often these Britons come up against linguistic and cultural barriers that they have not prepared for, and have, in response, clustered together away from the host society.

Most Britons who live abroad maintain strong ties and allegiances with the UK. However, these ties with home do not necessarily translate into a sense of collective identity while abroad. For a start, in life abroad national identities (particularly Scottish and Welsh) are far more prominent than a 'British' identity. Communities of Britons living abroad are also divided by factors such as class, duration of stay, and degree of integration into the host community.

New technologies are transforming the traditional links within British communities abroad and between them and the UK. The ability of individuals to stay in close contact with the UK via the internet, satellite telecommunications and cheap travel has perhaps reduced their dependence on meeting other British people overseas. It may also mean that there is less need for them to integrate into the host society.

Our research suggests that the UK will continue to experience high net emigration in coming years. If current trends continue, we could expect as many as a million more British nationals to emigrate over the next five years. In the longer term, if the UK's growing older population continues to show an eagerness for retiring abroad, we might see Britain's overseas pensioner population swell from the one million it is at present to around 3.3 million by 2050. This would inflate the amount of pensions being paid overseas to some £6.5 billion and healthcare payments to EU member states to £1.3 billion (in current values).

Most Britons who live abroad maintain strong ties and allegiances with the UK

Given the importance of emigration from the UK, this report suggests that UK policymakers should pay more attention to the issue. The UK government should follow the lead of several other countries and engage more with its diaspora. Such engagement would allow the UK to harness the potential of Britons living abroad to promote trade and investment links, develop overseas knowledge networks, and act as cultural ambassadors. More should also be done to promote the political participation of Britons living abroad and to make the most of returning Britons.

It will also be necessary for the UK government to devise fair and workable rules on how long and under what conditions a Briton living abroad is entitled to British public services. Such provision will not only ensure that those who are entitled to benefits receive them but will also help minimise the destitution experienced by some Britons living abroad who fall between the gaps of national entitlements. A better system of information on who is abroad at any one time will also be critical in ensuring the safety of Britons living abroad during times of crisis.

11 December 2006

➪ The above information is reprinted with kind permission from the Institute for Public Policy Research. Visit www.ippr.org for more information.

Britain's foreign-born population

The foreign-born population of the UK, 1951-2001 (as percentage of total population)

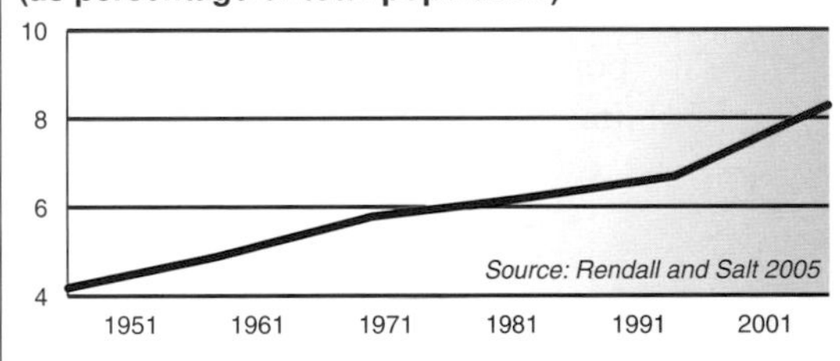

Employment status of working-age population by country of birth, excluding full-time students, 2005/06 (ranked by unemployment rate)

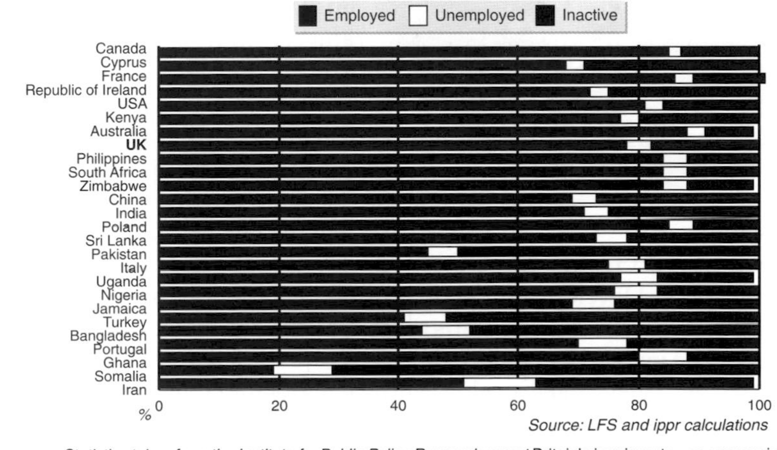

Statistics taken from the Institute for Public Policy Research report Britain's immigrants - an economic profile

Population estimates

UK population grows to 60.6 million. Information from the Office for National Statistics

In mid-2006 the resident population of the UK was 60,587,000, of which 50,763,000 lived in England. The average age was 39.0 years, an increase on 1971 when it was 34.1 years. In mid-2006 approximately one in five people in the UK were aged under 16 and one in six people were aged 65 or over.

The UK has a growing population. It grew by 349,000 people in the year to mid-2006 (0.6 per cent). The UK population has increased by 8 per cent since 1971, from 55,928,000. Growth has been faster in more recent years. Between mid-1991 and mid-2006 the population grew by an average annual rate of 0.4 per cent and the average growth per year since mid-2001 has been 0.5 per cent.

The mid-2006 population of the constituent countries of the United Kingdom is estimated as follows in the graph below.

The UK has an ageing population. This is the result of declines in the mortality rate and in past fertility rates. This has led to a declining proportion of the population aged under 16 and an increasing proportion aged 65 and over.

In every year since 1901, with the exception of 1976, there have been more births than deaths in the UK and the population has grown due to natural change. Until the mid-1990s, this natural increase was the main driver of population growth. Since the late 1990s there has still been natural increase, but net international migration into the UK from abroad has been an increasingly important factor in population change. In the year to mid-2006 natural change was an important driver of change accounting for 45 per cent of total change.

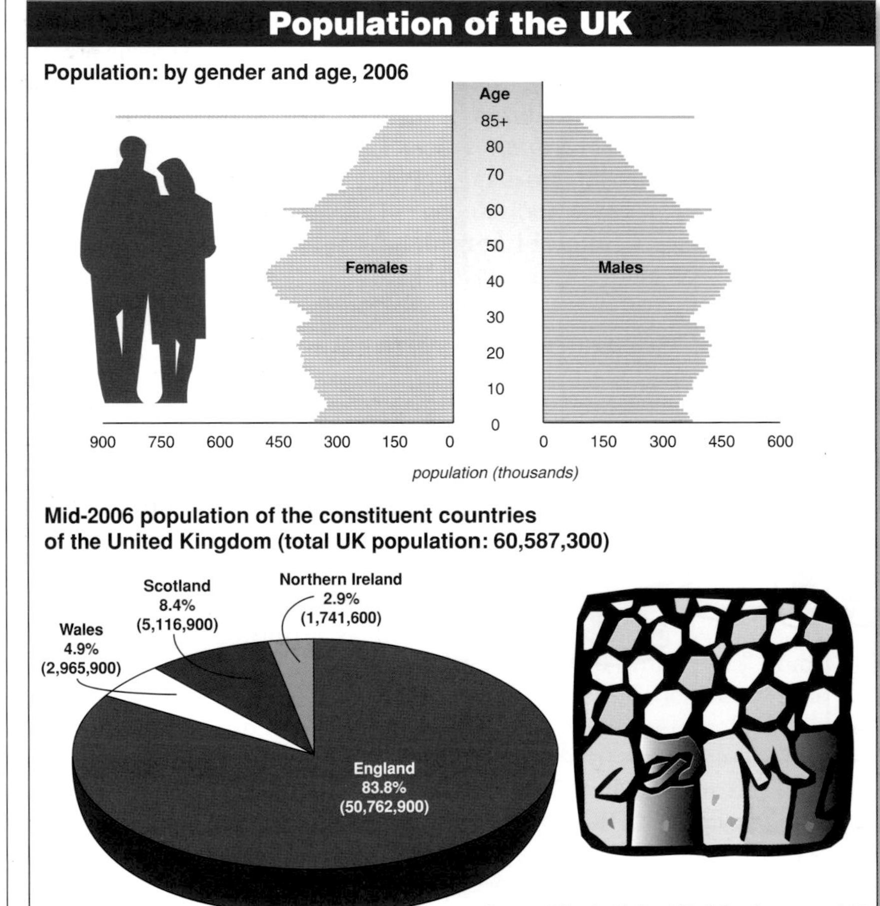

The UK has an ageing population. This is the result of declines in the mortality rate and in past fertility rates

Sources

Mid-year population estimates: Office for National Statistics, General Register Office for Scotland, Northern Ireland Statistics and Research Agency.

Notes

The average age of the population has been estimated using the median value. The median is the mid-point age that separates the younger half of the population from the older half.

Figures in the table may not add exactly due to rounding.

22 August 2007

⇨ The above information is reprinted with kind permission from the Office for National Statistics. Visit www.statistics.gov.uk for more information.

One in four UK babies born to a foreign parent

By Philip Johnston, Home Affairs Editor

One in four babies born in the UK has a foreign mother or father, official figures showed yesterday.

Population data for the year to July 2006 showed the proportion of babies born to a foreign parent has risen to 25 per cent compared to under 20 per cent just six years ago.

The startling statistic reflected the impact of recent record levels of immigration on the population.

A spokesman for the Office for National Statistics said: 'That reflects the cumulative effect of immigration over the last 40 years.'

Sir Andrew Green, the chairman of Migrationwatch, said over the next 20 years one in three new households will be a result of immigration.

'It is clear from these figures that immigration is continuing unchecked and continues to break all previous records – despite the fact this is opposed by the vast majority of the public,' he added.

Figures from the Organisation for Economic Cooperation and Development (OECD) earlier this year showed about six million people living in Britain – one in 10 – was born overseas.

This was far higher than the official figures from the 2001 census, which predated the recent surge in immigration.

Also, the foreign-born population is growing while the British-born population is declining. For almost a century, until the mid-1990s, natural growth was the main driver of population growth.

While there are still more births than deaths, net international migration into the UK has been increasingly important in population change.

The UK population has increased by eight per cent since 1971, from 55,928,000 to 60,587,000.

Growth has been faster in more recent years. Between mid-1991 and mid-2006 the population grew by an average annual rate of 0.4 per cent. The average growth per year since mid-2001 has been 0.5 per cent.

But this change has not occurred evenly across all age groups.

The population aged over 65 grew by 31 per cent, from 7.4 million to 9.7 million, while the population aged under 16 declined by 19 per cent, from 14.2 million to 11.5 million.

The largest percentage growth in population in the year to mid-2006 was at ages 85 and over (5.9 per cent).

The number of people aged 85 and over grew by 69,000 in the year to 2006, reaching a record 1.2 million.

This large increase reflects improving survival and the post-World War One baby boomers now reaching this age group.

The percentage of people under age 16 fell from 26 per cent in mid-1971 to 19 per cent in mid-2006. Over the same period, the percentage aged 65 and over increased to more than 11 million.

There is also a greater dependency of the old and young on the population of working age.

The proportion of babies born to a foreign parent has risen to 25 per cent

In 1971, there were 43.8 children per hundred people of working age, by 2006 this number had fallen to 30.5. This fall reflects both the smaller number of children in 2006 relative to 1971 and the increase in the working-age population, which was due to the 1960s baby boomers who joined the working-age population from the late 1970s. The ONS said the rise in the proportion of the population aged 65 and over is set to continue as the large numbers of people born after the Second World War and during the 1960s baby-boom age.

'As the baby boomers move into retirement they will be replaced in the working-age population by smaller numbers of people born since the 1960s,' the ONS said.

'Even though fertility has risen recently, the number of people being born is still less than was the case in the 1960s.'

24 August 2007

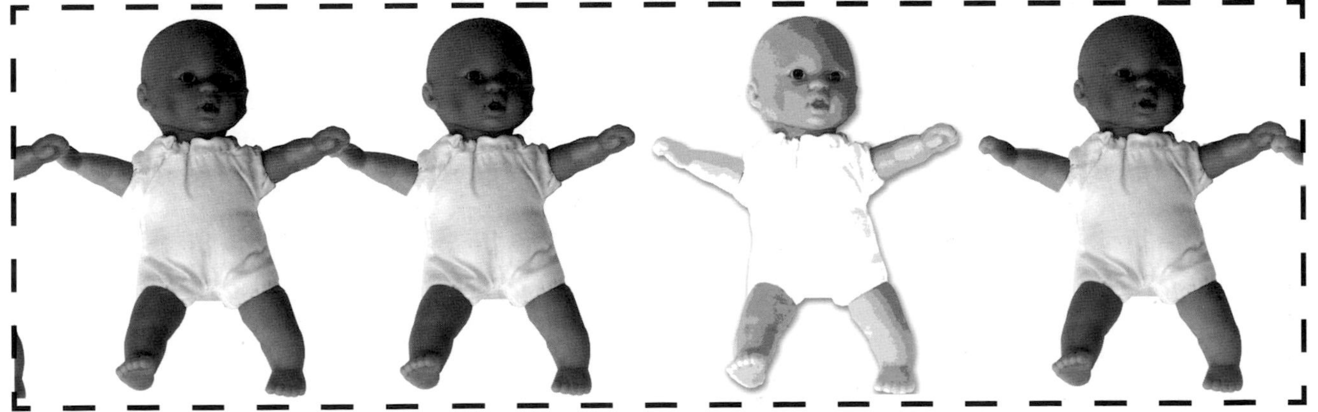

Prince, Davina and a baby revolution

The row over statistics showing 25% of UK babies are born to foreign parents overlooks a well-established trend, writes Esther Addley

The heir to the throne is one. The environment secretary, Hilary Benn, another. The television presenter Davina McCall a third. They are all among one of the UK's fastest-growing demographic groups – people born in this country whose mother or father was born overseas.

What these figures cannot tell us, crucially, is whether new parents who originated elsewhere will stay in Britain

More than a quarter of babies born in Britain have at least one foreign-born parent, it emerged this week, up from just over a fifth in 2000. It is a striking statistic that in some quarters, predictably, provoked alarm. 'Many people simply don't understand how this could have happened without anyone being consulted,' Sir Andrew Green, chair of the right-wing anti-immigration group Migration Watch, wrote in the *Daily Telegraph*. 'They are deeply concerned about the future.'

But a closer look at the figure, which emerged with the publication of the latest population data by the Office for National Statistics (ONS), suggests a more nuanced picture of the changing national demographic than is implied by the image of pramfuls of immigrant infants, screaming for British benefits.

'This figure appears striking, but it needs to be put in context,' said Richard Black, co-director of the Centre for Migration Research at the University of Sussex. The information does not tell us how many children non-UK-born parents will have, or indeed whether they will stay in Britain. 'What this shows is that there is a significant amount of immigration at the moment, and that immigrant mothers and fathers are still having children. That is all it shows.'

To many, of course, the figure of one in four is no great surprise. On any given day in her job, says Jane Hawdon, a consultant neonatologist at University College Hospital in London, 'you could work through an Atlas.

'It is impossible to give the full range of nationalities that I would encounter: Bengali, mothers from African countries, Turkish, Greek, eastern European of course, obviously English – and then there's the couple from Denmark who have come here for a weekend shopping and end up having their baby here.'

London is, of course, a special case: 51% of the 116,019 live births in the capital in 2005 were to a mother who was born overseas; in the wider south-east the figure was 17%. The data reveals disparities across England and Wales: across the north-east the proportion is 8%, in Birmingham 36%, in Forest Heath in Suffolk, where just 756 live births were recorded in 2005, 47% were to foreign-born mothers.

Notably, the increase across the country is not accounted for only by the UK's most visible immigrant groups. The number of babies born with parental origins in subcontinental Asia, Africa, the Caribbean and the far east increased from 44,103 in 1995 to 62,404 a decade later, but while the tally from Bangladesh rose from 6,783 to 8,217, those with origins in the EU (excluding Ireland) almost doubled to 20,420; the figures for the rest of Europe, at 7,504, were more than three times that of a decade previously.

At the heart of the debate is an undeniable rise in immigration to the UK in recent years, though without up-to-date census data it is difficult to put an accurate number on the rise. 'Of course, when you consider migrants, many are of the age where they are likely to become mothers or fathers,' says Peter Goldblatt, co-director of the ONS centre for demography. 'If you see an upturn in migration, as we have done in the past five to 10 years, this figure will be affected.'

What these figures cannot tell us, crucially, is whether new parents who originated elsewhere will stay in Britain. A significant proportion of recent births, for example, is accounted for by migrants from new EU countries such as Poland. But according to Mr Black: 'The obvious parallel to look at is the historical immigration from Italy or Spain or Portugal, and in all three cases the level of return has been quite substantial.'

However, there is no question that society is changing, argues Rick Muir, a research fellow at the Institute of Public Policy Research. He suggests that instead of considering ourselves an old, long-established and relatively static place, Britons must recognise that global mobility has made the UK, like so many other places, a mutable, energetic, changeable place, like young Australia or frontier America.

The challenge for policymakers, he says, is to encourage Britons to a more accurate understanding of their country. 'One thing the government has failed to do is to tell a story about the kind of society that we are today... which is one of multiple cultures and identities.

'Britain is now a place with diversity at its heart. With a few exceptions, it doesn't necessarily think of itself in that way. But that is what we are.'

25 August 2007

Baby shortage 'a myth'

Information from the Optimum Population Trust

The idea that the UK is suffering a shortage of babies and needs to boost its birth rate to prevent a future tax and pensions crisis is 'environmental and economic lunacy', the Optimum Population Trust said today (Monday, 20 February).

A report released yesterday (Sunday, 19 February) by the Institute for Public Policy Research, the leading New Labour think-tank, claimed there was a 'baby gap' of 90,000 between the number of children women say they wanted and the number they had. It said Britain was at a 'demographic fork in the road' and needed to increase its fertility to prevent future tax rises.

'The IPPR report says, in effect, that we need more babies to pay for our pensioners but this ignores the fact that those babies will eventually become pensioners themselves,' said David Nicholson-Lord, research associate for OPT. 'When that happens, we will need – on the IPPR's logic, at least – even more babies to support the even greater number of pensioners. Population would thus have to go on increasing ad infinitum – something the planet clearly cannot support.

The UK's population is projected to rise from over 60 million to nearly 71 million by 2074

'The IPPR just doesn't seem to understand the basic notion of environmental limits. In both economic and environmental terms, what they are proposing is lunacy. Maybe their researchers should get out a bit more and look at the devastating impacts on the planet that human population growth – even without the extra numbers they want us to produce – is already causing.'

Global population is forecast to rise by 40 per cent, from 6.5 billion to 9.1 billion, over the next four decades. In the UK – where the IPPR, in common with many politicians, claims we are facing demographic 'decline' – the population is projected to rise by 17 per cent, or 10.5 million, by 2074. The UK is already one of the world's most densely populated countries, with densities twice as high as those in China. Three-quarters of Britons think the country is overcrowded.

'The IPPR report takes only a few paragraphs to deal with environmental problems and reaches the stunningly complacent conclusion that "concerns about overall population size can be put to one side by British policymakers",' said David Nicholson-Lord. 'This not only discounts the direct effects of high population densities on quality of life and resources in the UK. It also ignores the fact that Britons are consuming around three times their share of the world's sustainable resources – and we'd need at least two extra planets if everyone lived a British lifestyle. A surge in the number of high-consuming Britons is one of the last things the planet needs over the coming century.'

OPT is calling for an international protocol on population to implement a sustainable population policy for the Earth. A 'population Kyoto' would set a framework in which the world could aim at population stabilisation and reduction targets, to be achieved through universally and freely available family planning, the encouragement of small families and balanced migration. On the basis of ecological footprinting research, it believes sustainable population targets would be 20-29 million for the UK.

Population facts

- The UK's population is projected to rise from over 60 million to nearly 71 million by 2074. This is equivalent to one and a half cities the size of London or 57 Lutons (population 184,000).
- If the current world population

stopped using fossil fuels and lived a western European lifestyle based entirely on renewable energy, it would still need, in total, 2.8 Earths – nearly two more planets – to support it, according to ecological footprinting calculations. To live within the carrying capacity of one Earth, population would thus need to be reduced by a factor of 2.8. In 2001, the year on which the calculations are based, a 'sustainable' world population would on this basis have been 2.2 billion – as opposed to the actual figure, 6.2 billion.

- The UK's 'ecological deficit' – the amount by which its global ecological footprint exceeds its own biologically productive capacity – is roughly 47 million hectares. This is roughly twice its land area (24 million hectares) and nearly three times its area of biologically productive land (18 million hectares). (*Living Planet Report*, 2004, WWF/UNEP.) In effect, we need between three and four UKs (3.6) to support its present population: most of the land used to feed and service the UK lies outside it.
- Projections commissioned by the OPT from the Government Actuary's department based on 2003 figures suggest that, with balanced migration and a fertility rate of 1.55 children per woman, the UK could lower its population to 53 million people by 2050 – 15-16 million, or over two Londons, fewer than projected. (The fertility rate is currently over 1.7.)
- Each Briton born today will 'consume' on average at least 2,780 tonnes of raw materials and natural resources in their lifetime. In weight terms, this is equivalent to over 360 red London (Routemaster) buses, around 1,080 sports utility vehicles (Range Rovers) or more than 278,000 mountain bikes. The figure excludes water. (Source: ONS, Environmental Acounts. The total material requirement of the UK economy was 2,112 million tonnes in 2004. UK life expectancy at birth is 79. A Routemaster bus weighs 7.6 tonnes, a Range Rover 2.57 tonnes, a mountain bike 10 kilograms.)

20 February 2006

- The above information is reprinted with kind permission from the Optimum Population Trust. Visit www.optimumpopulation.org for more information.

2007 world population

Information from the Population Reference Bureau

We entered the 21st century with 6.1 billion people. And in 2007, world population is 6.6 billion.

The increase in the size of the human population in the last half-century is unprecedented.

And nearly all of the growth is occurring in the less developed countries. Currently, 80 million people are being added every year in less developed countries, compared with about 1.6 million in more developed countries. While the less developed countries will keep growing, the more developed countries may grow slowly or not at all.

Population change is linked to economic development, education, the environment, the status of women, epidemics and other health threats, and access to family planning information and services. All of these factors interact with every facet of our lives, regardless of where we live.

It is remarkable that, despite many new developments over the past 50 years, one fact looks very much the same: Populations are growing most rapidly where such growth can be afforded the least.

Mortality rates

The phenomenal increase in population in the 20th century resulted from plummeting mortality rates, primarily in less developed countries. Advances in health and medicine that had taken many centuries to achieve in the developed countries spread quickly among developing countries. Even with the high death rates from HIV/AIDS, mortality has declined enough to fuel rapid population growth.

Life expectancy at birth rose rapidly and infant mortality declined sharply, narrowing the gap between rich and poor countries. In just 35 years, Costa Rica nearly closed its life expectancy gap with the world's wealthiest country – the United States.

The average life expectancy at birth in less developed countries rose from 41 years in 1950 to 66 years in 2007. The Middle East and North Africa region has experienced the largest increase in life expectancy since the late 1950s: from 43 years to 70 years.

Since 1950, the greatest gains in life expectancy at birth occurred among women. In more developed countries, average life expectancy for women rose from 69 years in 1950 to 80 years in 2007, while the average for men rose from 64 years to 73 years.

Fertility rates

A dramatic decline in fertility rates during the 20th century coincided with decreased child mortality, access to family planning, economic development, increases in girls' and women's education, and urbanisation. Other factors – including stiffer competition for jobs, housing shortages, and government efforts to lower birth rates – also encouraged fertility decline.

Fertility rates have fallen in every major world region, but in some regions, the rate remains quite high. Worldwide, the average number of children per woman fell from 5.0 around 1950 to 2.7 in 2007. Sub-Saharan Africa has the highest average at 5.5, falling from a level of 6.7 around 1950.

Couples were able to reduce family size by adopting methods of family planning. Worldwide, use of contraception rose from less than 10 per cent of married women of childbearing age in the 1960s to 62 per cent in 2007. Again, regional variations provide stark contrasts. In Africa, 28 per cent of married women use contraception; in Latin America, the share is 71 per cent; North America, 73 per cent; Europe, 67 per cent; and Asia, 66 per cent.

Foreign-born populations are rising in both industrialised and developing countries

Much press has been given to the increase in immigration in the industrialised world – most of which has come from developing countries. The United States and Canada, for example, both have long traditions of immigration, while many countries in western Europe have seen the influx of migrants from both former colonies in Asia and Africa (to the Netherlands) and eastern Europe (to Ireland). Less well known, however, is that several countries in the developing world have seen a rise in their foreign-born populations. Costa Rica, for example, has long attracted refugees escaping civil strife in nearby countries, and more recently has been a destination for Nicaraguans and Panamanians seeking seasonal work. Botswana provides another case in point, as it has attracted both refugees and economic migrants from its neighbours in southern Africa.

In Japan, 21% of the population is aged 65 and older. In Haiti, only 4% of the population is aged 65 and older

Urbanisation has grown dramatically since the 1970s

As recently as 1975, one in three persons worldwide lived in urban areas, with most of those 1.5 billion urbanites living in areas of fewer than 1 million persons. (Many urban dwellers, in fact, live in communities of fewer than 5,000 residents.) Over the past 30 years, the urban population has increased so that more than half of the world population will be living in cities by 2008. Parallel to this overall urban growth (and the continued rise of smaller cities) is the emergence of 'megacities' – urban areas of at least 10 million persons. Between 1975 and 2005, the number of such large cities has mushroomed from three (two of which were in industrialised countries) to 20 (15 of which are in developing countries).

Population ageing is occurring worldwide

Over the past half-century, both the worldwide drop in fertility and concurrent rise in life expectancy have led to the gradual ageing of the world's population.

Since 1950, the share of persons aged 65 and older has risen from 5 percent to 7 per cent worldwide. Europe led the way, with North America, Australia, and New Zealand close behind. However, older persons are now more than 5 per cent of the many developing countries and by 2050 are expected to be 19 per cent of Latin America's population and 18 per cent of Asia's.

September 2007

⇨ The above information is reprinted with kind permission from the Population Reference Bureau. Visit www.prb.org for more information.

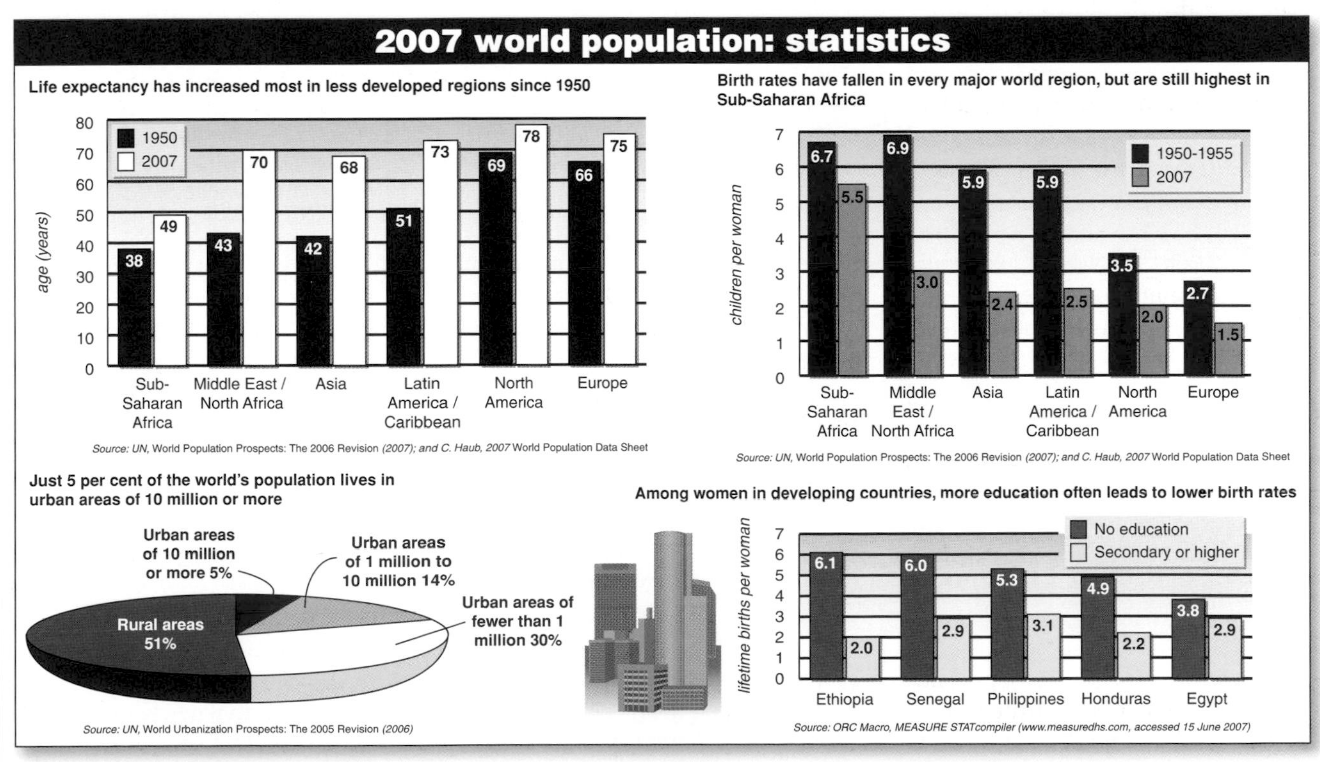

Population issues: meeting development goals

Information from the United Nations Population Fund

Reducing poverty and achieving sustainable development

- Population dynamics and trends, which are closely linked to economic progress, must be taken into consideration if the eight Millennium Development Goals (MDGs) are to be achieved.
- Ensuring access to sexual and reproductive health information and services, including voluntary family planning, is essential for achieving the MDGs, according to the UN Millennium Project.

The flow of financial resources to population activities

- The financial resources for the package of population and reproductive health programmes agreed to at the International Conference on Population and Development were US$17 billion by 2000 and $18.5 billion by 2005 – two-thirds from the countries themselves and one-third from the international donor community.
- In 2003, donors contributed about $3.1 billion, just 54 per cent of the donor commitment for 2000 and 51 per cent of the requirement for 2005. Domestic expenditures for the package in developing countries were estimated at $11.7 billion in 2003.

Population and poverty

- Some 1.2 billion people live in extreme poverty, on less than a dollar a day. Another 2.7 billion survive on less than $2 a day.
- 852 million people are chronically or acutely malnourished, some 300 million of them children. Every year more than 5.5 million children die of malnutrition-related causes.
- 114 million children do not get a basic education, and 584 million women are illiterate.
- The net increase in population is occurring in developing countries and, in many of them, the number of people living in poverty is rising.
- 350 million couples worldwide lack access to the full range of modern family methods and 137 million women would like to prevent or delay pregnancy but are not using any method of family planning.
- 40 million people are infected with HIV. In 2004 alone, some 3.1 million people died of AIDS, including 500,000 children under 15.
- If 15 per cent of a country's population is HIV-positive (a level nine countries are expected to reach by 2010), gross domestic product declines by about 1 per cent each year.
- The size, growth, age structure and rural-urban distribution of a country's population have a critical impact on development prospects and on living standards of the poor.
- The countries where poverty levels are highest are generally those that have the most rapid increases in population.
- There is substantial evidence that slower population growth and investments in reproductive health, HIV/AIDS prevention, education, women's empowerment and gender equality reduce poverty.

Population trends

- In mid-2005, world population was 6.5 billion people, 380 million more than in 2000. Currently, approximately 76 million people are added to the population every year.
- World population is expected to rise in the next 45 years by 2.6 billion, to reach a total of 9.1 billion in 2050.

The net increase in population is occurring in developing countries and, in many of them, the number of people living in poverty is rising

- The population of the 50 poorest countries is projected to more than double by 2050, and to at least triple in 12 of them.
- The overall population of the more developed countries will change little in the next 45 years, remaining at about 1.2 billion.
- Fertility rates are continuing to drop at the world level: in 1950-1955, the average woman had 5 children; in 2000-2005, the worldwide fertility rate was 2.65 children per woman; and in 2050, it is expected to be slightly over 2 children per woman.
- In the 50 least developed countries, fertility is 5 children per woman and is expected to drop by about half, to 2.57 children per woman by 2045-2050.
- A person born in 1955, according to the worldwide average, could expect to live to be 47. Now global life expectancy at birth

is 65, and is expected to keep on rising to reach 75 by 2045-2050.

- ➪ A child born today in the 50 poorest countries can expect to live on average to 51, and life expectancy by 2045-2050 is expected to be 66.5. In sub-Saharan Africa, life expectancy declined precipitously from 62 in 1990-1995 to 48 in 2000-2005. It is projected to decrease even further to 43 over the next decade.

World population is expected to rise in the next 45 years by 2.6 billion, to reach a total of 9.1 billion in 2050

Migration

- ➪ Some 175 million people, 3 per cent of the world's population, live outside their country of origin. That number is expected to grow to 230 million by 2050.
- ➪ Labour or economic migrants are the world's fastest growing group of migrants.
- ➪ Environmental degradation, exacerbated by population pressure, is a factor in both internal and international migration.
- ➪ More migrants are moving from poorer to richer nations, with an annual average of 2.6 million people going in that direction, about half of them going to Northern America.
- ➪ Women now constitute half of the international migrant population.
- ➪ During 1990-2000, 34 of the 44 developed countries were net receivers of international migrants. In 28 of them, migration either prevented population decline or contributed to population growth. During 2005-2050, the net number of international migrants to developed countries is projected to be 98 million.
- ➪ During 1990-2000, Asia was by far the largest source of migrants, followed by Latin America and the Caribbean, then Africa.
- ➪ Migrants send remittances to their countries of origin totalling at least \$90 billion a year, more than the \$60 billion developing nations receive in development assistance.
- ➪ An estimated 10.4 million international migrants are refugees. People internally displaced within their own countries number 20 to 25 million; many of them are increasing the numbers of the urban poor.

Population ageing

- ➪ Population ageing is an inevitable consequence of fertility decline, especially if it is combined with increases in life expectancy.
- ➪ The international community now views population ageing as a major development challenge, especially in settings where there is limited institutional, human and financial capacity to meet the basic needs of older persons.
- ➪ During the next 45 years, the number of persons in the world aged 60 years or older is expected to almost triple, increasing from 672 million people in 2005 to nearly 1.9 billion by 2050.
- ➪ Today 60 per cent of older persons live in developing countries; by 2050, that proportion will increase to 80 per cent.
- ➪ In developed countries, one-fifth of the population is 60 years or older; by 2050, that proportion is expected to rise to almost a third. In developing countries, the proportion of the older population is expected to rise from 8 per cent in 2005 to close to 20 per cent by 2050.
- ➪ The number of 'oldest old' people, those who are 80 years old or over, will increase from 86 million in 2005 to 394 million in 2050. By 2050, most oldest-old people will live in the developing world.
- ➪ In almost all societies, women represent the largest number and proportion of older people, even more so among the elderly.
- ➪ Today, just 11 developed countries have a median age of over 40. But by 2050, 90 countries will fall into that group, 46 of them in the developing world.
- ➪ Even as the global population ages, nearly half of all people today are under the age of 25 – the largest youth generation in history.

Urbanisation

- ➪ In 2007, for the first time in history, the majority of the world's population – 3 billion people – will be living in cities.
- ➪ During the next 25 years, the number of urban residents will increase by more than 2 billion people, while the rural population will decline by about 20 million.
- ➪ By 2030, two-thirds of the world's population will be living in urban areas. More than 90 per cent of this urban population growth will be in developing countries, and by 2030, all regions of the world will have urban majorities.
- ➪ Today there are 20 mega-cities of more than 10 million people, containing 4 per cent of the global population. By 2015, there will be 23 such mega-cities, 19 of them in developing countries.
- ➪ About a third of the world's urban residents, some 1 billion people, dwell in slums.
- ➪ Sub-Saharan Africa has the highest proportion of its urban population living in slums – nearly 72 per cent.
- ➪ The largest number of slum dwellers, 554 million people, representing 60 per cent of the world's total slum population, live in Asia, followed by Africa with 187 million (20 per cent) and Latin America and the Caribbean with 128 million (14 per cent).
- ➪ By 2030, close to 1.7 billion people in low-income and middle-income countries will be living in urban slums.

➪ The above information is reprinted with kind permission from the United Nations Population Fund. Visit www.unfpa.org for more information or to view references for this article.

Why we have a census

Information from the Office for National Statistics

We all use public services such as schools, health services, roads and libraries. These services need to be planned, and in such a way that they keep pace with fast-changing patterns of modern life. We need accurate information on the numbers of people, where they live and what their needs are.

Every ten years the census provides a benchmark. Uniquely, it gives us a complete picture of the nation. It counts the numbers of people living in each city, town and country area. It tells us about each area and its population, including the balance of young and old, what jobs people do, and the type of housing they live in.

Because the same questions are asked and the information is recorded in the same way

throughout the UK, the census allows us to compare different groups of people across the entire nation.

The census costs some £255 million for the UK as a whole, but the information it provides enables billions of pounds of taxpayers' money to be targeted where it is needed most. The census gives us invaluable facts about:

Population

An accurate count of the population in each local area helps the Government to calculate the size of grants it allocates each local authority and health authority. In turn, these authorities use census information when planning services within their areas.

Health

Data on the age and socio-economic make-up of the population, and more specifically on general health, long-term illness and carers enables the Government to plan health and social services, and to allocate resources.

Housing

Information on housing and its occupants measures inadequate accommodation and, with information about the way we live as households, indicates the need for new housing.

Employment

The census shows how many people work in different occupations and industries throughout the country, helping government and businesses to plan jobs and training policies and to make informed investment decisions.

Transport

Information collected on travel to and from work, and on the availability of cars, contributes to the understanding of pressures on transport systems and to the planning of roads and public transport.

Ethnic group

Data on ethnic groups help to identify the extent and nature of disadvantage in Britain and to measure the success of equal opportunities policies. The information helps central and local government to allocate resources and plan programmes to take account of the needs of minority groups.

Updated 1 March 2007

⇨ The above information is reprinted with kind permission from the Office for National Statistics. Visit www.statistics.gov.uk for more.

What is a census?

Since 1801, every ten years the nation has set aside one day for the census – a count of all people and households. It is the most complete source of information about the population that we have. The latest census was held on Sunday 29 April 2001.

Every effort is made to include everyone, and that is why the census is so important. It is the only survey which provides a detailed picture of the entire population, and is unique because it covers everyone at the same time and asks the same core questions everywhere. This makes it easy to compare different parts of the country.

The information the census provides allows central and local government, health authorities and many other organisations to target their resources more effectively and to plan housing, education, health and transport services for years to come.

In England and Wales, the census is planned and carried out by the Office for National Statistics. Elsewhere in the UK, responsibility lies with the General Register Office for Scotland and the Northern Ireland Statistics and Research Agency.

Peering into the dawn of an urban millennium

Information from the United Nations Population Fund

In 2008, the world reaches an invisible but momentous milestone: for the first time in history, more than half its human population, 3.3 billion people, will be living in urban areas. By 2030, this is expected to swell to almost 5 billion. Many of the new urbanites will be poor. Their future, the future of cities in developing countries, the future of humanity itself, all depend very much on decisions made now in preparation for this growth.

While the world's urban population grew very rapidly (from 220 million to 2.8 billion) over the 20th century, the next few decades will see an unprecedented scale of urban growth in the developing world. This will be particularly notable in Africa and Asia where the urban population will double between 2000 and 2030: that is, the accumulated urban growth of these two regions during the whole span of history will be duplicated in a single generation. By 2030, the towns and cities of the developing world will make up 81 per cent of urban humanity.

Urbanisation – the increase in the urban share of total population – is inevitable, but it can also be positive. The current concentration of poverty, slum growth and social disruption in cities does paint a threatening picture: yet no country in the industrial age has ever achieved significant economic growth without urbanisation. Cities concentrate poverty, but they also represent the best hope of escaping it.

In 2008, for the first time in history, more than half the world's population, 3.3 billion people, will be living in urban areas

Cities also embody the environmental damage done by modern civilization; yet experts and policy-makers increasingly recognise the potential value of cities to long-term sustainability. If cities create environmental problems, they also contain the solutions. The potential benefits of urbanisation far outweigh the disadvantages: the challenge is in learning how to exploit its possibilities.

In 1994, the Programme of Action of the International Conference on Population and Development called on governments to 'respond to the need of all citizens, including urban squatters, for personal safety, basic infrastructure and services, to eliminate health and social problems...' More recently, the United Nations Millennium Declaration drew attention to the growing significance of urban poverty, specifying, in Target 11, the modest ambition of achieving by 2020 'a significant improvement in the lives of at least 100 million slum dwellers'.

UN-Habitat's Third World Urban Forum, as well as its *State of the World's Cities 2006/7*, successfully focused world interest on the deteriorating social and environmental conditions of urban localities. The process of globalisation has also drawn attention to the productive potential of cities and to the human cost. Yet the enormous scale and impact of future urbanisation have not penetrated the public's mind.

So far, attention has centred mostly on immediate concerns, problems such as how to accommodate the poor and improve living conditions; how to generate employment; how to reduce cities' ecological footprint; how to improve governance; and how to administer increasingly complex urban systems.

These are all obviously important questions, but they shrink in comparison with the problems raised by the impending future growth of the urban population. Up to now, policymakers and civil society organisations have reacted to challenges as they arise. This is no longer enough. A pre-emptive approach is needed if urbanisation in developing countries is to help solve social and environmental problems, rather than make them catastrophically worse.

The present Report thus attempts to look beyond current problems, real, urgent and poignant though they are. Yet, it is also a call to action. The Report tries to grasp the implications of the imminent doubling of the developing world's urban population and discusses what needs to be done to prepare for this massive increase. It looks more closely at the demographic processes underlying urban growth in developing areas and their policy implications. It specifically examines the consequences of the urban transition for poverty reduction and sustainability.

It surveys the differing conditions and needs of poor urban women and men, and the obstacles they face as they strive to claim their rights and realise their potential as productive members of the new urban world.

Although mega-cities have received most of the attention, conditions in smaller urban areas call for even greater consideration. Contrary to general belief, the bulk of urban population growth is likely to be in smaller cities and towns, whose capabilities for planning and implementation can be exceedingly weak. Yet the worldwide process of decentralising governmental powers is heaping greater responsibility on them. As the population of smaller cities increases, their thin managerial and planning capacities come under mounting stress. New ways will have to be found to equip them to plan ahead for expansion, to use their resources sustainably and to deliver essential services.

One of the Report's key observations is that poor people will make up a large part of future urban growth. This simple fact has generally been overlooked, at great cost. Most urban growth now stems from natural increase (more births than deaths) rather than migration. But wherever it comes from, the growth of urban areas includes huge numbers of poor people. Ignoring this basic reality will make it impossible either to plan for inevitable and massive city growth or to use urban dynamics to help relieve poverty.

Once policymakers and civil society understand and accept the demographic and social composition of urban growth, some basic approaches and initiatives suggest themselves. These could have a huge impact on the fate of poor people and on the viability of the cities themselves. Throughout this Report the message is clear: urban and national governments, together with civil society, and supported by international organisations, can take steps now that will make a huge difference for the social, economic and environmental living conditions of a majority of the world's population.

Cities concentrate poverty, but they also represent the best hope of escaping it

Three policy initiatives stand out in this connection. First, preparing for an urban future requires, at a minimum, respecting the rights of the poor to the city. As Chapter 3 shows, many policymakers continue to try to prevent urban growth by discouraging rural-urban migration, with tactics such as evicting squatters and denying them services. These attempts to prevent migration are futile, counter-productive and, above all, wrong, a violation of people's rights. If policymakers find urban growth rates too high, they have effective options which also respect human rights. Advances in social development, such as promoting gender equity and equality, making education universally available and meeting reproductive health needs, are important for their own sake. But they will also enable women to avoid unwanted fertility and reduce the main factor in the growth of urban populations – natural increase.

Secondly, cities need a longer-term and broader vision of the use of urban space to reduce poverty and promote sustainability. This includes an explicit concern with the land needs of the poor. For poor families, having an adequate piece of land – with access to water, sewage, power and transport – on which they can construct their homes and improve their lives is essential: providing it requires a new and proactive approach. Planning for such spatial and infrastructure requirements, keeping in mind poor women's multiple roles and needs, will greatly improve the welfare of poor families. This kind of people-centred development knits together the social fabric and encourages economic growth that includes the poor.

Similarly, protecting the environment and managing ecosystem services in future urban expansion requires purposeful management of space in advance of needs.

The 'urban footprint' stretches far beyond city boundaries. Cities influence, and are affected by, broader environmental considerations. Proactive policies for sustainability will also be important in view of climate change and the considerable proportion of urban concentrations at or near sea level.

Thirdly, population institutions and specialists can and should play a key role in supporting community organisations, social movements, governments and the international community in improving the nature and form of future urban expansion, and thus enhancing its power to reduce poverty and promote environmental sustainability. A concerted international effort at this critical time is crucial to clarify policy options and provide information and analyses that will support strategies to improve our urban future.

⇨ The above information is reprinted with kind permission from the United Nations Population Fund. Visit www.unfpa.org for more information or to view references for this article.

Ageing population

Information from Age Concern

In the United Kingdom, in 2005, according to estimates based on the 2001 Census of Population, there were more than 11 million people of state pension age and over (11,244,000):

- 9,381,000 in England;
- 975,000 in Scotland;
- 609,000 in Wales;
- 280,000 in Northern Ireland. (1)

In 2005, the population of the United Kingdom, based on mid-year estimates, was 60,209,000. Of this figure, 18.7% were over pensionable age:

- 7,100,000 were women aged 60 and over (of whom 5,505,000 were aged 65 and over);
- 4,143,000 were men aged 65 and over;
- 9,647,000 were people aged 65 and over;
- 4,599,000 were people aged 75 and over;
- 1,175,000 were people aged 85 and over. (2)

A man of 60 could expect to live for another 20.5 years and a woman of the same age for 23.6 years, based on data for the years 2003-2005. (3)

It is projected that by mid-2007, in the United Kingdom, 11,000 people will be aged 100 and over. (4)

Looking at the minority ethnic population in the United Kingdom, in 2001, within specific groups:

- 11% of Black-Caribbean people were aged over 65
- 2% of Black-African people were aged over 65;
- 7% of Indian people were aged over 65;
- 4% of Pakistani people were aged over 65;
- 3% of Bangladeshi people were aged over 65;
- 5% of Chinese people were aged over 65. (5)

The number of people over pensionable age, taking account of the increase in the women's state pension age, is projected to increase from nearly 11.4 million in 2006 to 12.2 million in 2011, and will rise to over 13.9 million by 2026, reaching over 15.3 million in 2031.

The change in state pension age for women will be phased in between 2010 and 2020 and will not affect anyone born before 6 April 1950. (6)

According to estimates, 75% of those aged 65 and over voted at the 2005 General Election compared to 37% of those aged 18-24. (7)

The number of people over pensionable age is projected to increase from nearly 11.4 million in 2006 to 12.2 million in 2011

Sources of data used

1) *Population Trends* (PT 126) 126, Winter 2006, National Statistics © Crown Copyright 2006, table 1.4 (Population: age and sex). www.statistics.gov.uk/downloads/theme_population/PopTrends126.pdf
2) PT 126, op cit, table 1.4 (Population: age and sex).
3) Interim Life Tables, Office for National Statistics (ONS) © Crown Copyright (Expectation of life, United Kingdom, males, based on data for the years 2003-2005); (Expectation of life, females, based on data for the years 2003-2005). www.gad.gov.uk/Life_tables/docs/wltukf0305.xls www.gad.gov.uk/Life_tables/docs/wltukm0305.xls (06/03/07)
4) Population projections by the Government Actuary, United Kingdom. Projected populations at midyears by age last birthday, 2004-based, The Government Actuary's Department (GAD) © Crown Copyright 2005. www.gad.gov.uk/Population/2004/uk/wuk04singyear.xls (06/03/07)
5) *Social Trends 2006*, 36, National Statistics © Crown Copyright 2006, table 1.5 (Population: by ethnic group and age, 2001 Great Britain).
6) National population projections 2004-based, National Statistics © Crown Copyright 2006, table 3.2 (Actual and projected population by age United Kingdom 2004-2031). www.statistics.gov.uk/downloads/theme_population/PP2_No25.pdf
7) The growing importance of older voters: an electoral demographical model for analysis of the changing age structure of the electorate, by Scott Davidson. Loughborough University, 2006. www.20millionvotes.org.uk/reports/electoral_demography_report.pdf

➪ The above information is reprinted with kind permission from Age Concern. Visit www.ageconcern.org.uk for more information.

Will the UK struggle to cope with the effects of an ageing population?

KEY FACTS

➪ Migration is not a recent phenomenon. For centuries, people have moved across borders for economic and political reasons. (page 1)

➪ Half of all international migrants are women, often leaving their children and families behind, and mostly engaged as domestic labour. (page 2)

➪ 76% of people in Great Britain surveyed by Harris Interactive felt there were too many immigrants in their country. (page 3)

➪ The term migration refers to the movement of persons between countries for the purpose of taking up residence. (page 4)

➪ In 2004 144,000 migrants came to the UK for work-related reasons. (page 4)

➪ 39% of people granted settlement in the UK in 2004 originated in Asia, with 28% from Africa and 19% from Europe. (page 5)

➪ On 22 July 2006 the Home Office released figures showing that 427,000 people from new EU member states have registered to work in the UK since May 2004. (page 6)

➪ 16% of new immigrant workers were earning below £5 an hour in 2005, compared to 9% of all immigrant workers and 10% of UK-born workers. (page 8)

➪ Between 50,000 and 80,000 of eastern England's 2.8 million economically active people are migrant workers, contributing about £360m a year to the economy, according to research from the East of England Development Agency (EEDA). (page 12)

➪ 683,000 migrants have applied to work in Britain from Eastern Europe since 2004, but the rate is slowing. In the second quarter of 2007, applications fell to 50,000, which is 6,000 lower than the same period in 2006. All but 3% are employed and 56% say they plan to stay for under three months. (page 13)

➪ In a recent opinion poll 76% said that they favoured an annual limit on immigration. Only 10% were opposed. (page 16)

➪ In a poll earlier this year, 47% of the British people insisted migration had been bad for the economy. (page 18)

➪ Theoretically, migration can be seen as a simple process that consists of three phases: where a person comes from, where they are going, and where they end up. (page 21)

➪ Those who are settled in the UK can bring dependent members of their family to the UK. In 2004, approximately 34,230 family members joined British citizens or persons previously granted settlement. (page 23)

➪ Over the 39 years between 1966 and 2005, the UK experienced a total net loss of some 2.7 million British nationals. In other words, every year for the past 39 years, around 67,500 more British nationals left the UK than came back to it. (page 24)

➪ IPPR research suggests that around 5.5 million British nationals live overseas permanently (equivalent to 9.2% of the UK's population). (page 24)

➪ Much migration is the consequence of areas becoming degraded through environmental damage, says the Optimum Population Trust. There are an estimated 30 million environmental refugees. (page 26)

➪ In mid-2006 the resident population of the UK was 60,587,000, of which 50,763,000 lived in England. The average age was 39.0 years, an increase on 1971 when it was 34.1 years. In mid-2006 approximately one in five people in the UK were aged under 16 and one in six people were aged 65 or over. (page 28)

➪ One in four babies born in the UK has a foreign mother or father, official figures have shown. (page 29)

➪ Global population is forecast to rise by 40%, from 6.5 billion to 9.1 billion, over the next four decades. In the UK the population is projected to rise by 17%, or 10.5 million, by 2074. (page 31)

➪ Currently, 80 million people are being added every year in less developed countries, compared with about 1.6 million in more developed countries. (page 32)

➪ Worldwide, use of contraception rose from less than 10% of married women of childbearing age in the 1960s to 62% in 2007. (page 33)

➪ In developed countries, one-fifth of the population is 60 years or older; by 2050, that proportion is expected to rise to almost a third. In developing countries, the proportion of the older population is expected to rise from 8% in 2005 to close to 20% by 2050. (page 35)

➪ Since 1801, every ten years the nation has set aside one day for the census – a count of all people and households. It is the most complete source of information about the population that we have. The latest census was held on Sunday 29 April 2001. (page 36)

GLOSSARY

Accession
Increasing the size or extent of something with new additions.

Affluence
Abundant wealth or resources.

Brain drain
When skilled workers leave their own country, usually to go somewhere with better economic and social opportunities.

Brownfield
Previously developed, often contaminated land, with the potential to be redeveloped.

Consumption
Use of goods and services.

Correlation
A relationship between two seemingly independent things.

Demographic
Population characteristics.

Dependants
Individuals dependent on another in terms of housing, food, money etc. Dependants might commonly include children still living at home, elderly relatives or a non-working partner.

Embarkation
The process of boarding a ship, plane, or train.

Empirical evidence
Evidence which depends on sensual observation – knowledge based on what one can touch, smell, taste, hear or see.

Ethnic group
People identified with one another, usually on the basis of sharing a common religion, nationality or ancestry, which sets them apart from the majority.

Expatriate
A person residing in a country from which they don't hold a passport.

GDP (gross domestic product)
The value of all the goods and services produced in a country in a year.

Greenfield
Previously undeveloped land.

Grey economy
A market in which goods are sold and bought without the authorisation of the manufacturer.

Integration
Becoming part of something.

Linguistic
Language-related.

Persecution
Mistreatment or harassment of an individual or group, generally due to their beliefs.

Political asylum (or right of asylum)
The legal right of a person persecuted in one country for their political or religious beliefs to be protected by another country.

Quota
A specific, limited number of something.

Ratification
Formal process in which a signatory (usually a country) agrees to be bound by the conditions of a treaty.

Redeployment
Assignment of people to a different task or job.

Remittances
Transfers of money by foreign workers to their home countries, usually through their families.

Resident
Living at a particular place.

Social cohesion
When a society works together for shared values and rights.

Trafficking
The illegal buying, selling and moving of people or goods.

Transferable skills
Abilities and knowledge that can be applied in more than one job or career.

Transit
Passing through somewhere on the way from one place to another.

Xenophobe
Someone with a fear or hatred of foreigners or strangers.

INDEX

Additional Resources

Other* Issues *titles

If you are interested in researching further some of the issues raised in *Migration and Population*, you may like to read the following titles in the ***Issues*** series:

- Vol. 147 *The Terrorism Problem* (ISBN 978 1 86168 420 2)
- Vol. 146 *Sustainability and Environment* (ISBN 978 1 86168 419 6)
- Vol. 131 *Citizenship and National Identity* (ISBN 978 1 86168 377 9)
- Vol. 120 *The Human Rights Issue* (ISBN 978 1 86168 353 3)
- Vol. 115 *Racial Discrimination* (ISBN 978 1 86168 348 9)
- Vol. 110 *Poverty* (ISBN 978 1 86168 343 4)
- Vol. 107 *Work Issues* (ISBN 978 1 86168 327 4)
- Vol. 105 *Ageing Issues* (ISBN 978 1 86168 325 0)
- Vol. 98 *The Globalisation Issue* (ISBN 978 1 86168 312 0)
- Vol. 89 *Refugees* (ISBN 978 1 86168 290 1)

For more information about these titles, visit our website at www.independence.co.uk/publicationslist

Useful organisations

You may find the websites of the following organisations useful for further research:

- **Age Concern:** www.ageconcern.org.uk
- **AVERT:** www.avert.org
- **Economic and Social Research Council:** www.esrc.ac.uk
- **Harris Interactive:** www.harrisinteractive.com
- **Institute for Public Policy Research:** www.ippr.org
- **Migration Watch:** www.migrationwatch.com
- **Office for National Statistics:** www.statistics.gov.uk
- **One World:** www.oneworld.net
- **OpenEurope:** www.openeurope.org.uk
- **Optimum Population Trust:** www.optimumpopulation.org
- **Population Reference Bureau:** www.prb.org
- **Trades Union Congress:** www.tuc.org.uk
- **United Nations Population Fund:** www.unfpa.org

ACKNOWLEDGEMENTS

The publisher is grateful for permission to reproduce the following material.

While every care has been taken to trace and acknowledge copyright, the publisher tenders its apology for any accidental infringement or where copyright has proved untraceable. The publisher would be pleased to come to a suitable arrangement in any such case with the rightful owner.

Chapter One: Migration and Security

Migration guide, © December 18/OneWorld.net, *British least supportive of immigration*, © Harris Interactive, *Migration in the UK*, © Economic and Social Research Council, *Migration from Bulgaria and Romania*, © Open Europe, *Migration facts and figures*, © Trades Union Congress, *Has migration led to unemployment?*, © Trades Union Congress, *Frequently asked questions*, © Migration Watch, *Police chief warns of migrant crime impact*, © Telegraph Group Ltd, *What about a welcome amid the warnings?*, © Guardian Newspapers Ltd, *Human rights of female migrants*, © United Nations Population Fund, *Outline of the immigration problem*, © Migration Watch, *Irrationality grips the British concerning migrants*, © Guardian Newspapers Ltd, *Does migration hurt migrants?*, © Trades Union Congress, *HIV, immigrants and immigration*, © AVERT, *Improving population statistics*, © Crown copyright is reproduced with the permission of Her Majesty's Stationery Office, *Brits abroad*, © Institute for Public Policy Research, *Mass migration damaging the planet*, © Optimum Population Trust.

Chapter Two: Population

Population estimates, © Crown copyright is reproduced with the permission of Her Majesty's Stationery Office, *One in four UK babies born to a foreign parent*, © Telegraph Group Ltd, *Prince, Davina and a baby revolution*, © Guardian Newspapers Ltd, *Baby shortage 'a myth'*, © Optimum Population Trust, *2007 world population*, Population Reference Bureau, *Population issues: meeting development goals*, © United Nations Population Fund, *Why we have a census*, © Crown copyright is reproduced with the permission of Her Majesty's Stationery Office, *Peering into the dawn of an urban millennium*, © United Nations Population Fund, *Ageing population*, © Age Concern.

Photographs

Flickr: page 17 (carnalvalet).
Stock Xchng: pages 13 (Suzi Fenton); 18 (Sanja Gjenero); 22 (Martin Walls); 26 (Sachin Ghodke); 34 (mokra); 36 (B S K); 37 (Chris Jewiss); 39 (Nate Brelsford).
Wikimedia Commons: pages 29 (AJ); 38 (Jonathan McIntosh).

Illustrations

Pages 10, 19: Don Hatcher; pages 12, 24: Bev Aisbett; pages 14, 21: Simon Kneebone; pages 16, 31: Angelo Madrid.

Additional research and editorial by Claire Owen on behalf of Independence.

And with thanks to the team: Mary Chapman, Sandra Dennis, Claire Owen and Jan Sunderland.

Cobi Smith and Lisa Firth
Cambridge
January, 2008